I0438360

# WE CAN'T STAND
# FOUR MORE YEARS...

Written by

Michela Hawkins

# DEDICATION

I am dedicating this book in the memory of my parents, my family, and to Glenn Beck and the Fox News Network.

Many thanks to the media coverage you have offered your viewers over the years. Although it isn't always pleasant or popular, at least it is presented as fair and balanced as possible.

You have taught me more about the America I live in than any teacher or book could possibly have taught me. Thanks so much for that education. You have been a true inspiration to me. I feel I have progressed from being one of many "not so informed" housewives and mothers to someone who can carry herself in reasonably intelligent manner in conversations with others.  Until I was divorced and had to worry about my own finances, I never realized just how important having this knowledge could actually be to me.

# INTRODUCTION

This book is meant to be an easy read. It was written, hopefully, to try to raise your awareness of the way our lives may be drastically changing, right before our very eyes, by the events that are happening around us today.

We have to change the direction we are heading before it's too late. If we don't, merely accepting the alternative is not good. I felt a real urgency to tell everyone they need to wake up and get informed. Time is running out.

I have no degrees to speak of nor am I famous for anything I have done. I felt I had this mission to try to touch you in some way and get you into action. We are in a war here in the United States whether you know it or not. You need to be alert. You need to know it isn't over yet, that there is possibility for change to happen. There is hope for us, but only if we act now.

I hope you will find this as informative and thought provoking. I hope my attempt at humor brings a smile to your face, maybe making you think about what America was like and how it can be again. Now sit back and humor me by reading this.

# TABLE OF CONTENTS

## Chapter One

<u>THE UNITED STATES OF AMERICA?</u>

**W**hat have they done with my America?  What's happening to it? I really am beginning to wonder where the heck I am living? Do you get that same puzzled feeling? Or am I alone? I have a feeling I'm not.

Geez.. I guess it's still alright to call it  America. Or is that now politically  incorrect? Maybe I should have said the Collective States of Immigrants and Natural Born Citizens. Well, I guess that doesn't take into consideration of the illegal aliens, too.  What do you call us anymore? If you look at the way our elected officials are acting then you can't even say "United States."

Just look at what's happening in the battle of the states trying to overturn the Health Care Plan, Obama Care.  Just how many dollars are we all going into debt just to try to keep from implementing Obama's Health Care Plan?

Someone's paying for all the attorneys to fight this. Of course, it will be coming out of your pockets. And look how much time is being spent to just to try to fight the program. It's absurd. I'll get into that later.

When I was in high school we had a lot of Cubans who defected and moved into our area. Now we're talking about small town America in the 1960's. Florida was just a natural jump off for defections from Cuba. You remember the Cuban Crisis don't you? We lived with the fear that we may get bombed by nukes and blown off the face of the earth between the Russians and Cubans. That was frightening for us. Castro was another "spooky dude" to use a favorite description often used by Fox News' Glenn Beck to describe George Soros. I think Castro was a real spooky dude.

Back to the teachers I was talking about. They were wonderful people. They came into Florida legally and instantly became model citizens. He was an attorney in Cuba and I don't recall what she did, but their kids were very friendly and eager to become part of our township. Almost everybody loved them.

I can remember when I was happier to see a new ethnic restaurant open up in my neighbor-hood. It was fun to sample new and different foods and meet new people. I still like to do that. Maybe somehow that won't get ruined, too.

We had Spanish Clubs, French Clubs, and Latin Clubs in our school. I still remember taking Spanish and managing to learn enough to get by if I ever had to speak the language. You learned a little about their cultures, too, and that made it interesting and fun.

Oh, we had a lot of migrant workers, too, but because they were seasonal, you didn't get to know them well. Usually they lived on the property they were working in very tiny houses that were supplied to them. They usually stayed to work in the orange groves as pickers or in the fields to pick crops. You never heard of them causing any problems. They were there to work and they worked hard. You ever been in the Florida sun all day bent over? But, they were grateful for the work, not like today.  They weren't looking to sue somebody or join Unions or cause problems in town. It was a tough way to live, but it beat what they came from in comparison.

Back in those days, listen to me I sound ancient, you learned English first even though it sounded a little like Florida Cracker English! Then a second language, of our choice, was required for graduation.

It was sort of expected that if you came to live here from some other country that you would learn to speak English. It was just the way things were done. If you wanted to live in the States you needed to be able to converse with the majority of the population. They

3

were expected to fit into our society not the other way around. And you know what, nobody complained. They were anxious to "fit" in.

Nowadays you hear the most ridiculous, absurd incidences coming from our schools. One kid was questioned by the CIA because he made a comment on Facebook about Bin Laden. The gist of what he was saying was that Obama better be careful because Bin Laden might do something to us even though he is dead. He was questioned without his parents being there. That wasn't right. Do you really think this young man is a threat to us? More than likely, he had over-heard conversations about what might happen to us now because of the death of Usama Bin Laden. Kids don't get it all correct. They should have been assuring that kid that it will be alright, that we are all keeping watch out to make sure that nothing is happening. Kids are scared today. It's my opinion, mind you, I don't know the kid personally, but I don't think he meant harm.

What about the recent story of the older kids, at a teacher's meeting, chaining themselves to chairs and chanting a message about how they feel we stole the property from the Mexicans? Can you believe that one? Who's behind this type of behavior? Would you ever dream of acting like that in your school? Not me.

4

Kids have gotten in trouble over saying the Pledge of Allegiance and saluting the Flag. Excuse me, is this America? When I was in school, we started our day out saying the Pledge of Allegiance to the Flag. The Flag was an integral part of our routine and was honored. I never heard of anyone complaining that they had to say the Pledge. In fact, even though our class-rooms were multi-ethnic, I never heard of a single complaint of any kind. We were all proud to be Americans no matter where we came from, it was a given.

There was a big ruckus about the Flag the other day because on Flag Day some people were offended that their flag wasn't, also, displayed. Another kid got in trouble for wearing a tee shirt that had an American Flag on it.  Good grief! What happened to being proud of our flag and our heritage?

There's a story happening now that a graduation ceremony is being held up until the ONE person who objects to having the ceremony in the Church where it has been held for many years takes down its cross. ONE person is objecting. I'm sorry, but shouldn't the majority rule on this?  This one person should maybe have had a private graduation ceremony in another location and let the other kids enjoy their tradition. I know I will catch heat over that, but that's the way I feel. That's how I was brought up. If you are the one that is unhappy then you don't ruin it for everyone else. I'll bet you ten to one that one person's kid would be happy if the parents just went along with the group. Don't you know that kid will be alienated and taunted about the way it is being handled? I wouldn't want to be in his shoes. I probably wouldn't want to go at all after all this trouble.

Don't get me wrong, I do believe that everyone has a right to his own opinion and to their own beliefs. At what point do you have the right to trample all over everyone else's beliefs and on traditions though?

If that had been my kid, I would have asked him if he would like to invite some guests privately to celebrate his graduation and I would have done my own thing. After all, when you go to graduation you can only invite so many people anyway. I'll lay you odds that kid probably would have liked that just fine.

At school events, if you didn't want to do something, you just didn't. You didn't call reporters and make the headlines because you found an issue to be able to sue some-one over or be able to complain about. I think there is much ado about nothing most of the time until someone eggs somebody else to start a new cause.

6

Have you heard some of the stories about what they are teaching our kids nowadays? If I were a parent in today's times, I would be more concerned about what's being taught. It was recently exposed in a news story that some schools were actually touting Marxism and Socialism instead of teaching what the meaning of democracy and the traditions and our heritage that has been to us. I don't think Civics is being taught any more.

Also, there was a recital at a school where the kids were talking about boycotting companies in a song produced for this program. That was on Fox News not long ago. Holy cow! I want my Grandkids to be taught exactly what is the Bill of Rights, the Declaration of Independence and what the Civil War was about and what the Constitution means. What happened to our teaching history and what made the United States a country to be proud of and to celebrate?

Our children are the future. Should our children be taught that if you own a big company, you should first establish union rules and have collective bargaining? Or should they be taught that you must earn your place out in the job force and ask to negotiate certain privileges on your own? Should they be informed that they may not be getting what they pay for if they join a union? Look at what's been happening on the news lately with the Teacher's Union. Why should some teachers be kept on the payroll when they aren't earning their way? There are bad teachers out there ruining it for the good, dedicated ones that do care.

Oh boy, now the Unions will be after me, too. I definitely believe that Unions have their place, but they have gone too far, too. Originally, unions were formed to protect workers and their rights and that was a good thing. Now they have turned into huge lobbyists persuading and contributing to our politicians for political gains and favors. Promises made or huge pensions and entitlements that we can't afford to keep doing are made on a regular basis.

I volunteered for many years to be an aide in my son's school. Then, all the sudden, you weren't allowed to help anymore. Maybe I wanted to see how they were treating the children and what they were teaching them. That ended that! Then you heard about how the teachers couldn't get their work done during normal hours. They had help but stopped it. Why didn't they just leave it alone? The mothers who volunteered didn't mind doing it.

There are good , dedicated teachers out there and they far out number the ones who should have been fired. I do appreciate those dedicated ones. They

8

work hard and care thast the students are trained and should be rewarded.

Everything has changed so much. Is it better? I don't think so. Somewhere along the line things went off track, ideals changed.

Are our kids learning what a democracy is really about? Are they learning what our true rights are according to the Constitution and the Bill of Rights? Do they have any idea what a privilege it is to be able to attend school every day unlike children in third world countries? Are they being taught that?

I don't think we keep a close enough eye on what our kids are doing either. Between what they are being taught in schools, the after care programs, too much to do once the family is home, and the stress of just being a kid today, we have a big problem. It's probably become a combination of all of that.

Remember when we had school sponsored field trips to some great attractions? What fun they were and they usually were to some wonderful places to teach us about our environment or about some historical event. I always loved school. I don't think school is "fun" any more. Kids don't refer to going to school as being fun nowadays. I don't think it is.

The schools have changed, too. The new curriculum for teaching is different, the school books are different. Even the lunchroom is changing. Granted we do have obese children, but is it that Physical Education is not being required or is it that the kids are being offered the wrong choices? Is it that we are all out there so busy just trying to make ends meet that we can't worry about what they are eating. Now the government wants to control the lunchrooms, too. By no means do I think that the government should be in control what your kids eat. What my child puts in his mouth is my responsibility not someone else's. We have enough control from the government.

Truthfully, I would not want to be a kid in these times. It isn't that we didn't have issues to deal with back then , but the kids don't have good news any more. Day after day they all get bombarded with news about countries fighting each other, riots, how broke our country is and that we are on the brink of financial disaster.

They get in trouble for saying what they think it isn't what the day's politically correct thing to say might be. They get into trouble with the clothes they wear. Heaven forbid if they should wear red, white and blue or have a biblical quote on their tee shirt! They get expelled for that.

Can't we do it like we did in the past? Can't the child who doesn't want to say the Lord's Prayer or salute the flag or say the Pledge of Allegiance just not say it? Can't they sit quietly by and let the rest of the students say it? It isn't that we aren't aware their religion may be different or their beliefs might be different, it's that this is what our country was founded upon and we should be allowed to applaud this and celebrate this. I would never make anyone say the Lord's Prayer if they didn't really want to participate, but I would appreciate that they would let me. Whose country did they move to for all these rights? Why did they come here if they hate our traditions and our ways so much?

We have gone so far overboard with this correctness that I don't even know if I am allowed to introduce myself as Ms. Hawkins anymore. There just has to be a way to be proud of being an American without being chastised for it. The Constitution was meant to be a guideline for all of us to live by and as a reminder to us all to live with integrity in what we do. Where's the integrity of the people gone? Are we getting to be afraid to speak our minds because we may get beat up for it? Isn't this the land of the free and don't we have the right to freedom of speech and some independent thought? Why is it so hard to do that? As I write these words, I am thinking how I will have a whole variety of people chastising me because I have made a comment they don't like. I'm not going to apologize for anything I say. It's my own personal opinion, but there are a lot of people that agree with me.

One thing I have always prided myself in is that I feel I have great integrity. My parents have brought me up to appreciate that everyone can have their own opinion. I respect that, and yes I am a bit opinionated, but at what point do we say the majority rules? Why do the majorities have to suffer because of what one or two others don't like?

I was watching the news the other day and it was almost comical when the commentator was trying to relay a message. Three separate times he started over with corrections of words he was using. He even laughed. It's getting to be absurd! This just has to change!

Why do we have to walk on eggshells and try to please every single person living in our own country? Are we so afraid of some sort of retaliation that we don't dare show our true colors of how proud we are of this America, the land of the free? I think we have just gone way overboard.

Chapter Two

## HAVE YOU BEEN SHOPPING LATELY?

In the sixties it seemed like everything was made in Japan. It used to be there or from the Philippines. Now, lately, have you picked up something that isn't made in China? Most of the food is from another country. What happened to Made in America? Maybe I don't shop in those stores because they are too expensive for me. Hmmm.

Donald Trump was saying on the news the other day that he would bring America back to America. Although he has many dealings with the Chinese he says they don't respect us. He says they laugh at us, all the way to the bank. He said he would be happy to do business in America if we would be somewhat competitive in the business market and offer what it is he is buying from them. How sad it is that we have lost our desire to produce merchandise here or that we have "taxed" ourselves out of the chance to make it here.

We have the highest corporate taxes in the whole world now. How can we expect any our businessmen to set their businesses locally when they are taxed to death here? We all know that the "cheaper" products are being produced abroad. Is it that we have gotten so greedy to make the buck that we will not take less profit to have it be made in America? Or is it that we have become just a little more complacent letting someone else make it? You know it's kind of like eating a tv dinner rather than fixing a meal. It's easier.

It is disheartening when you read that General Motors and, heaven only knows, how many other companies paid no taxes this year. Explain to me why was it they needed a bailout? Was it to be able to pay all those pensions and those big executive salaries? I don't get it.

Maybe we have just a few too many tax credits for the big companies. If they are making that kind of profit then maybe they could pay less for corporate taxes, but get less in tax credits. I forget which politician made that suggestion but I thought it had merit. It is probably much too logical or practical to consider.  I know it has been discussed numerous times only to be discussed again with no resolve.

No, I am not against big business either. Don't get all over me about that. The very backbone of America is based upon our businesses and I realize that and appreciate it. With big business comes big lobbying, too, though. Small businesses create jobs, too.

How many political favors have been given in return for a some consideration? How many times has corruption been exposed from big business? Our news is full of it.

I think about my own personal taxes. I inherited, through a very messy divorce, a number of properties that went into default within three months of my divorce. We are talking about almost a million dollars in properties. I have hundreds and hundreds of thousands of dollars in losses. How come I can only claim $3000 a year? I can't live long enough to collect the tax credits on these properties. Should General Motors who makes billions of dollars in profit be allowed more credits than I should get? How is this fair?

In addition, I have been paying the taxes on these properties, too. Some of them I haven't even gotten back in foreclosure yet. What's wrong with this picture?

Definitely, our taxing system is broken and needs some revamping. It has to be more fair for everyone.

Do I think someone who has started a business and made it a success should be taxed more? No, but maybe to be taxed differently. What we're doing now isn't working well. We need to bring our businesses back home.

The Mom and Pop business can't manage to keep up with the economy either. It used to be that if you started a business you had a chance to build it up before they hit you with a lot of taxes. The days of true entrepreneurship are pretty much over. Many of our restaurants are falling by the wayside at a huge rate. They always did have a bigger attrition rate, but not like today.

You know when the big chain stores are closing up and cutting back that the little guy doesn't stand much of a chance. People are afraid to try to start a new business because they can't afford to fail. The risk is too great for most of us. The internet has hurt a lot of local businesses because there is no foot traffic anymore. It's easier to shop the internet.

Have you walked into a mall lately? Did you notice how many stores are closed up? Nobody's walking around with an armful of packages from merchandise they just bought. Nobody can afford to,  so they shop on the internet and get it delivered. You see a lot of mall walkers. Believe me, it isn't cheap to get into a large mall either. You usually have rent, a fee for advertising, and sometimes a percentage of your profits. Not just anyone can afford all that. Of course, since the housing crisis, rent has come down a little. What good is that when there's no one shopping?

How about the grocery market? Have you noticed how prices just keep slipping upwards? Check out the packaging, too.  Companies like a popular juice maker have shaved off a few ounces of juice to make the pricing look better. They certainly aren't alone. Lots of companies are re-packaging. It's one way to make you think you aren't really paying more. It's pretty smart marketing on their part.

One of our local food markets, Publix, has a lot of these "buy one get one free" sales. Boy, I load up on them when I can use the product. Thank you, Publix. I am one very appreciative shopper.

Come to think of it, I really don't see the amount of shoppers in there I used to see either. It's that way everywhere. A couple of our food markets have closed here already. Even our local Super stores are not as full of shoppers. I know they have become serious competition for the neighborhood markets, but they aren't that busy either. Are many people having to drastically cut the food budget to trade off for gas? I think so. I know I have and I'm a typical consumer.

I just about choked when I filled up my car one time a few weeks ago. I had to stop at $50.00 and then pump again. I stay home most of the time so I let it run lower then fill up when I'm out buying groceries or whatever. I'm one of those people who drive so little each year that I get a reduced milage rate on my car insurance premium. Thank goodness, the bank and grocery store are close to my home.

You hear that all the speculators in gas commodities are running the price of gas up one minute then the next you hear it's because we aren't using as much oil and the demand is down so price goes up. I wonder what the truth really is? I can't understand why oil drops, but our gas prices don't. Hmm. Makes you wonder.

Drill, Baby, drill.  I'm with Palin on that. Why aren't we using our resources? Supposedly, we have more oil than any other country. Well, what are we waiting for? I don't like being at the beckon call of the Middle East. We aren't liked there. We aren't respected there. They are raping us. And what kills me is that we give them billions of dollars in aid for the right to rape us. Wouldn't it be wonderful to be able to become self sufficient? What about the Keystone Pipeline? Why wouldn't we agree to that? We need jobs and oil.

Recently, President Obama made a trip to Brazil and announced that we have pledged  billions of dollars for their drilling explorations. He, also, said that we wanted to be their best customers. Huh? I haven't talked to anyone who thought this was a good idea. Why  the heck aren't we paying for our own drilling explorations? Heck, we already know where the darn oil is, why don't we do it here?

Oh yea, because of the big oil spill. Yes, that was a terribly tragic event and yes, many lives were changed because of that spill.  Hey, I have two of my wonderful properties in Milton just miles from Pensacola. That oil spill made the sale of those places impossible and rental, forget it. Nobody wants to even look. So I do have an interest in the spill and I did lose because of it. That area will be down for years.

Maybe it was because somebody was so busy making money, they got lackadaisical about checking the back up support systems and cut corners. Did I think all drilling should be permanently stopped forever? No. I think that closer attention to safety measures and more rigorous checks ought to be made. The jobs created by our drilling alone would help revive the local industry. I'm a native Floridian, too. I think it can be done responsibly.

I often wonder if the closing down of the rigs had anything to do with trying to force us to buy cars that were fuel free. Isn't that just great when Obama says for all of us to go buy electric cars? Don't you just love it? I can't afford the car I've got more over have the money to buy a new one. They aren't cheap you know. When they can make one for $10,000 call me. Why is it that we can go to the moon and beyond, but can't build a car for the average American can afford? Don't they realize that if cars were cheaper then we would probably trade out more often?  Oh, don't tell me they can't do that because it would cost them too much to produce it. Tell me it's because they don't want to make less profit. Be honest about it.

There's that Chinese car that, compared to ours, is somewhat affordable. Forget it! They own us now.

What happened to the ethanol program? Oh, that's right, we are using up our crops to make ethanol. These are the same crops that have risen dramatically in price. These are the same crops we are shipping overseas to feed every nation that says it's hungry. How many people, in the U.S. do we have on food stamps now?

Oh, geez, now I hate everyone in starving nations. No, I don't. Wait a minute, didn't we clone some sheep and a mule? Why the heck can't we clone a bunch of chickens, cows, etc. ,show them how to clone them, and keep them fed? Maybe the whole entire world's problems shouldn't be ours alone either. That's a fascinating thought. Maybe our 17% that we contribute to the United Nations for funding should be spread around a little more fairly. There are people starving in America, too.

I wonder if anyone ever thought of moving those people in the starving nations to more fertile land and teaching them how to take care of themselves? That would be a novel idea, I'm sure. How about some of the richer nations pitching in some more? Does the phrase "physician heal thyself" mean anything we should be thinking about? How many Americans are on Welfare?

Look how many crops are being ruined from flooding in some parts of the US and drought in others. Isn't that a little scary when you think about all that we are shipping out? These crops are ruined. Just maybe we should stop paying farmers to NOT grow crops and let them grow all they can. I've always thought it was ridiculous and a real rip off to pay people not to grow crops. How about the people who put one cow on a lot and call themselves a dairy? That's a crock, too. Oops, I think a large entertainment park in Orlando does that for a huge tax credit. Well, I guess you can't blame them for working the system. Everybody else does.

I live in a deeded residential area where you can't plant anything without asking for the permission of the Home Owners Association to do it. I'm fine with that myself. I don't want to be in a neighborhood where the people in the house next door can decide to paint their home purple with blue shutters. OK, I didn't ask if I could grow my tomatoes. They are inside a screened lanai and they are in two pots. I'm doing pretty good keeping them growing. I may be planting a lot of other things if groceries get too much more expensive.

Truth is, I have been stocking up on canned goods a little at a time as my budget can afford to do it. I am sad to think that the day may come when I will be happy I did this. And yes, I bought extra dog food, too. Believe me, if I get hungry enough I will be fishing out of the pond in my back yard. Something tells me it's not a bad idea to stock up.

What a shame it is that these things have become such a worry. I can recall the stories my grandparents told me about the big depression. Of course, I really couldn't relate to them then. Now I am beginning to understand that you can't have whatever you want to put in your grocery cart. I'm beginning to understand it more now. I am praying it doesn't get to be worse each month. I fear it will.

You know what I just realized? I haven't been shopping just for "fun" in over a year. If I don't just absolutely need it, I don't buy it. Well, that's not exactly true, the difference is that I can't afford to buy it anymore. Shopping used to be fun, a social event, now it's only by necessity. A lot of us shopped for fun. Actually, it's probably a good thing I did because I am now wearing those clothes that I shopped for and bought years ago. They are going to have to last.

Dinner out? Nope. I don't eat out unless it's a date and they are paying for it. Eating out was such a wonderful social thing to do, but when you don't go out to eat that shoots that. Buying food and fixing it at home isn't cheap either. I had my son, daughter-in-law, and my two grandkids over the other day for my daughter-in-law's birthday. The chicken alone was $21.00. Geez! Thank goodness, we are a small family. I don't know how larger families feed a hoard.

I just caught the news on the update from all the tornadoes, storms, and droughts going on here in America. What a tragedy these people are going through. Mother Nature can be very cruel.

I made a donation to the Red Cross. There's not much else I can do to help them, but something like that. It really irks me when I hear that Obama is going to "rehab" Tunisia and Libya and donate a billion or two to them. What about our displaced American families here? Are you helping them?

If we could afford to be "taking care of" the world my attitude would be totally different. We need to get ourselves in shape here first! This just has to change. And I'm not against helping starving nations overseas either, but do we have to be the bread basket for the world?

## Chapter Three

## WHAT ABOUT OUR SERVICEMEN?

There isn't anyone in this world who supports the efforts of our servicemen more than I do. My Grandfather was a Colonel in the USAF and my Dad served in both the RAF and the USAF. Many of my family members have served and served proudly. The walls in my office have some wonderful pictures of them.

Even though I didn't understand the Viet Nam War, I supported our troops who were there. I lost many classmen from my high school due to that war.

Please explain to me why we are in all these Middle Eastern and African countries? These people hate us and we have given them billions of dollars for all that hate. My Dad used to say you can't buy love. Our government has forgotten that lesson. We are hated abroad.

I understand why we would be supportive of Israel even though Obama slapped them in the face with "his proposals" to go back to 1967 borders. I can certainly understand why we were very supportive to the Saudis because of the oil there. Oh yea, we paid them to be our friends, too. I'm sure they just love us to death.

Please tell me why we are paying Pakistan? Is it so they can buy more nuclear weapons to perhaps use against us? You know darn well they knew Osama Bin Laden was there. I'll never believe they didn't. They are not our friends.

I think we should pull most of our troops from Afghanistan and Pakistan. In fact, maybe move them over to the border in Israel. I don't think we should be meddling in their affairs. This fighting between the Israelites and the Palestinians and has been going on for eons. Since when does a President decide how another country should be divided?

I realize that there was going to be a genocide in Libya if someone didn't do something. We sure dragged our feet long enough on that one. The Middle East looks like another long "termer" to me though. Of course, if you're leading from behind it's different. We get exactly what we deserve there when we defray and procrastinate the way we did.

Sometimes you should let things work themselves out without interference. Did anyone ask for our help? Meanwhile, many billions of dollars later, the Middle East and Northern Africa are on fire.

Where's the Saudi support? It's in their backyard

literally. They have enormous funds to contribute. Why aren't they helping? Donald Trump called that one right, too.

I hate to sound so mercenary, but really America can't solve its own problems right now. What are we doing overseas? It doesn't mean we will never be a supportive country again. It just means for now, until we get back on our feet. Our economy means everything to the world. So why aren't we concentrating on it?

Obama was in Ireland not long ago. Oh great, now he's  promising them money. NO. NO. I have to live on my budget. Let them figure out how to live on theirs. Greece, Portugal, and Spain…you, too. I might want to spend my money differently! Why do I have to pay for their over-spending?  Nobody pays for mine.

I wish that Obama would give some very serious consideration to all the spending he has allowed to happen. He's never been on a budget. He's rich! Make him live off of $2000 a month and I'll bet he couldn't do it.

He's so busy campaigning right now and doing a world tour that he doesn't really have time to be a President. I know I'm picking on him, but, guess what gang, he's our President. It is happening on his watch!

I have another bone to pick with him, too. How many trips have we as the taxpayers of America paid for in order for Obama to go campaigning? Do you know what the security alone must cost? How about the fuel for those two Air Force One jets? How about the transportation of everyone who accompanies him on these trips? Is that coming out of his campaign fund? I seriously doubt it!

In the first place, I don't think that the President, not only Obama, should be allowed to campaign at all. Why should he? He's had four years to prove his worthiness as the leader of the nation. If we don't know what he represents by then we won't ever know. His record ought to be substantial enough for his running in the next election.

By the way, what we pay our troops is shameful. How about all the foreclosures that have been done while they are serving overseas?

I think it is horrendous that they have to go into battle worrying about whether their family is getting kicked out of their home or not. I personally know people who have not made a payment in two years and they are still living there. Come on guys, give the troops a break.

I do like the "draft" idea especially as part of the immigration process. If they have to fight for their right to live in America, then maybe they would be more appreciative of the rights they receive. Maybe they would understand what it is we are fighting for a little better.

I say bring the majority of our troops home and put them on our South-western borders. That would give them a job, help keep illegals out of the US, and provide some safety for the Americans who live in these areas. Allow them to ask questions and to shoot back. What good is a gun is you can't use it to protect? Our own borders need to be secure.

Sure, you hear all about the corruption in the border people. Hey, you get caught you go to jail. No early negotiations for time off. The drug lords will get real tired of being shot at, too. Anyone caught entering illegally gets a chance to go serve in the military in a totally different arena. It would be just like our current government to put them guarding the border. Duh! It's just got to stop. They need to speak English, too. I don't care where they come from as long as the will go through the process.

29

Do you want to know what I heard coming from an adjoining room in the hospital emergency ward once? The young girl in the next bed said to her friend. "I thought I was going into labor". The friend with broken English said, that she should have waited until she was sure. She said she has all her babies paid for by the emergency room. My Dad and I just looked at each with great disgust. She continued on to tell the ER clerk that she had no insurance. But of course, she also, was in such a hurry to get there that she didn't have her Driver's License with her . She probably gave a false name and address. She had only her friend to see her through this.

How many hundreds of thousands of illegals have come into the States just to have their kid and then get their kid taken care of his whole life on our tax dollar? I heard the number the other day and the cost of this care was almost unbelievable.

My Grand-daughter was financed when she was born. We made a lot of jokes about whether they would repossess her if they didn't keep making their payments. She's worth every dime!

Look at what's happening in the news right now with the legal arguments from the Americans wanting to go to college who are being penalized, often turned away, so that illegals are going to school either free or on a very reduced cost instead of these kids. I would be ticked off, too.

I managed to go one and a half years to college on a Scholarship Loan that I paid back in full. I had to go to work at the beginning of my second year or I would have continued my education. I had to self educate from there. I was appreciative for what I did complete. I earned it myself.

The program for schooling after you serve in the military is phenomenal. What a great opportunity for citizens who want to become legalized to be able to take advantage of after they serve. There are lots of programs for help with education. You have to want to do it for yourself

In my opinion, there ought to be an accelerated income for any servicemen with special duties. Would you want to serve your time in a desert where behind every bush is someone who wants you dead? I know I sure wouldn't. They deserve more pay. It would make joining the service much more appetizing if the pay was increased.

Another bone I want to pick is if you're sending troops into a zone you know is booby-trapped to the ninth degree and that your actual chances of getting blown up or shot are almost a given, then give the troops all the protection you can. Give them the equipment they need. Would you want to go fight a war with a slingshot? Me either.

The battles should be chosen carefully. It's time we pick and choose better where we want to go and what we are there for in return. War is very expensive, not only with the lives lost but monetarily. I'm not anti-war. I just think we ought to know why we are there. Our policy ought to be clear cut.

Trump once said that we should end up with the spoils when we fight. I have to say, I kind of agree with him. We end up spending billions of dollars to rebuild nations that absolutely hate our guts. This makes no sense to me at all.

Am I the only one that thinks Obama should give back the Nobel Peace Prize? What exactly did he do to earn that? I'm really foggy on that.

Remember, I don't hate our President. I just think that he's doing a lousy job on his watch. Am I better off today than when he took office? Good Lord, no. I'm not even close. I'm terrified what the next few years will bring.

One of my biggest fears is that we are going to witness the beginning of World War III. The total unrest in the Middle East and Africa is enough to worry about by themselves. This disease is spreading from one country to another. Europe is no exception. There were riots in Greece, Great Britain, France, and many other nations. There is no peace in the world. I pray it isn't so and that it doesn't come to pass. I'm really concerned that it will.

Look at what's happening in North Korea now and we know they have nuclear capabilities. We have witnessed that. Let's hope they are not out to prove how powerful they are even though they are a small country. We wouldn't want them to recklessly use their weapons. We know they have biological weapons at the border, too. Their army of over a million active soldiers could be formidable.

A friend just asked me where would I live if I had plenty of money to be able to live very comfortably. My answer is here where I am now. No matter how bad things get, I still have hope for America to keep from becoming a third world nation.

One of the financial advisories I subscribe to made a comment the other day that I should have a safe place to go if things get really bad here in the States. He went on to describe where he and his family would go until "things" get better.

Where would that be? What's to guarantee that wherever he's talking about wouldn't change, too? I at least live under laws here that, although some aren't great, I can at least depend on to keep me safer.

Have you heard of the massive movement, usually done as secretly as possible, to take old missile silos and salt mines and turn then into storage for DNA and seed banks? Have you heard or seen some of the documentaries about colonies that are being built to sustain hundreds of people at a time in case of a disaster? These are being built all over the world with only the wealthiest of clients eligible to have a spot in them. They have been built deep inside caves and in underground bunkers. They are built to withstand radioactive bombardment or catastrophic natural events, anything from nuclear war to a super nova. Isn't this frightening not to know what they know?

The world's not a safe place anymore with all the unrest everywhere, the radical people and religious fanatics. I can't think of a single place outside the United States where I would feel totally at ease now.

To be honest, one of the best times I ever had in my life was the six weeks I spent in Europe. It was the trip of a lifetime. I had done some traveling to Europe before, but this was the best trip. A friend went with me and we went everywhere by train. We made one reservation and that was for a room in the airport for the day before we were to leave. Everyone was friendly and happy. I never once felt threatened anywhere.

There is no way I would travel overseas at this point. I know there are places that would maybe have been safe, but some of those places have had terrorist attacks, too. I certainly wouldn't travel by ship either. What a shame that our world has become such a place of danger and despair. There are so many beautiful countries to visit. No way I would make that trip now.

I took a whole bunch of cruises to the Caribbean and the Islands, Mexico, too. Not any more. Especially Mexico at this point. These parents that let their kids go to Mexico for spring break are nuts to let them go there.

What is another shame is that now I want to go all over the States to see the National Parks I haven't seen and a whole list of cities I want to visit. Now I not only wouldn't feel safe in some of those states, but I can't afford to go. All these demonstrators, the Occupy groups, etc., would make me think twice about going anywhere they were. That really sucks. My driving trip to the Grand Canyon got cut down to a day at the beach here.

It's just got to change! Our children will never have the world at their feet like we did. We have to try to make things better for them, for our grand children.

## Chapter Four

## YOU SPENT HOW MUCH?

I don't know of anyone who isn't very aware of the impending debt crisis we are now facing. Except for Obama maybe, who seems to be able to ignore it and keep on spending. I thought he was supposed to be so bright. How can an intelligent human being not see where we are heading? He doesn't listen to his own advisors. Why? There must be s good reason for this, but I sure can't think of what it might be.

First off, I would like to know who he is listening to for advice? I sure hope that the eight or nine visits, the recorded ones that we know of, from George Soros would not be on his list of "favorites." I am very concerned about why our President is allowing a man who has verbally announced that he is going to take us down financially would even be allowed in the White House. Soros visits Hillary, too.

Believe me, this is a reason for close scrutiny and a round of questions for an explanation of why Soros is a guest in our nation's capital. Why is he there? That may be where some of Obama's funding might be coming from, or at least a good part of it. I hope full disclosure of campaign funds is enforceable. I want to know how much influence has been bought. Obama has the media behind him. That influence bought by the media is directly because of the funding from Mr. Soros. Does that make you nervous? It should.

On the Glenn Beck Show, it was pointed out how many organizations this man has in his command. The stock market business channel ,also, said that Soros was a huge shareholder in Petrobras. He sold his shares just before our President visited Brazil to tell them we will give them billions. I understand that Soros bought back his many shares after that was a public announcement. By the way, Petrobras stands for petrol Brazil. Hmm. Interesting?

Back to the budget. How on earth did we get by without having a budget in place anyway? Do you know of anyone who can run a household or any business without having a budget of some kind? How do you know how much you've spent if you don't know what your accounting says?

I don't have much money so I have to keep close track of it. Maybe that's the difference. When you can just print more what difference does it make? Don't you wish you could print more when you need it?

There is something that really bothers me a lot. My

understanding of the Federal Reserve in a nutshell is this. Originally, it was started by five wealthy business-men. These men held one quarter of all the wealth of the entire world. You know like the Vanderbilts, the Rothchilds, JP Morgan. Their meeting was held very secretive because they were mostly bankers, imagine that! They didn't want the nation to think they were just out or themselves. Somewhere along the way the ownership became even more secretive. Now, mind you, the Federal Reserve does not work for the Government. They answer only to their owners. A list of potential Chairmen is given to the Government to choose from as to the Board. Bernanke is the current Chairman of the Federal Reserve. He answers to no one but the Reserve.

In the past, the Federal Reserve has bailed the US out of trouble. We are talking about an incredible amount of money supposedly in the Reserve. The Reserve has been buying Treasury Notes to the tune of about 70% of our total indebtedness. China owns the majority of the rest. The Reserve has already said it will finish out Quantitative Easing 2, but was not going to do a QE3. In his infamous speech to the Nation, he also, said they weren't planning on buying any more notes. The Reserve has never opened its books to public scrutiny. Remember, it answers to no one. There have been many theories that there is no

39

gold in the Reserve. When money is needed they just print more. It's all digital anyway.

What if the Reserve decides to sell its Treasury Notes to Russia or someone else? What if they raise our interest rates to where they can't be paid? Then the owners of the Federal Reserve own the United States of America. Is that as frightening to you as it is to me? What if George Soros was one of the owners of the Reserve or one of the Buyers of our notes? George Soros has announced that he wants a New World Order. This would be a Socialistic New Order. Does this sound familiar? Is history repeating itself? Germany once had a leader with these kind of aspirations. Look what happened. Now are you a little worried or at least interested to learn more for yourself?

There is a "club", a secret society, that meets for two weeks every year in California. Membership is quite expensive and is kept as anonymous as possible. Recently a reporter gained access by sneaking in and hiding. Mind you, this is a very closely guarded area called the Bohemian Grove. It's a large amount of acreage that is patrolled and guarded. There are no women members. Local people are brought in to handle the catering needs of the group.

Why do I mention this? I mention this because it is said that the most powerful, influential men in the world meet there. It is said, there is a ceremony performed on a stage at the beginning of their secret meeting. Dinner is served. Then discussions begin among the membership. These discussions are said to include what the next step is to bring about the New World Order. They decide who does what and where it needs to be done. I'm not happy thinking that some leader from another nation has any influence over what my country will be like in the future or that we are being manipulated without our knowing it. Just look it up on the internet, shuffle past the denials that it is a "harmless" fun vacation, and notice that this is happening all over the world.

Our country needs transparency alright because we sure haven't gotten any so far. Let's face it. All those behind door meetings with men who publicly have stated that they will bring us down by creating this New World Order should be thoroughly investigated and addressed for an explanation.

Have you noticed the Stock Market lately? Holy cow, it's all over the board. Commodities have soared mostly up. Gold and silver have dropped then have started coming back. One day, even during one market day, you start off with a sell off and the next the market can do no wrong. People don't know what to do with their money. We are all running scared. The dollar drops and gold goes up. I feel for the financial analysts because there's no rhyme or reason to anything. They can't explain or predict why the market is so crazy either. Personally, I couldn't do the roller coaster ride. I sold out and went to precious metals and a rental home.

There sure have been a lot of insider cases lately, too. That sure does rock your confidence as an investor. Everybody seems to be out for themselves. There's that greed again.

Politicians, in general, have taken a real beating lately, too. I'm sure there are a dedicated few, but it seems harder to find them. The lobbyists ruin the politicians. I'm so sick of the Democrats fighting with the Republicans and vice versa. Forget being re-elected and concentrate on the job you are supposed to be doing.

I can't believe that Obama is never around to get down to solving the Economic woes of our country. He's off to campaign or vacation or whatever. I have never seen a man travel so much. Shouldn't he be home addressing the    issues like our finances? I would love to know how much has been spent on his travels. Maybe he figures he might as well stretch it as far as he can because he may not be re-elected. I don't know. You've got me on that one. If I really felt like his many trips are all warranted then it would be different. I just wish he would make the appearance of actually running the government,  and being our Commander in Chief, our fearless leader. Am I alone in this? I think not. The polls say differently.

His decision to take out UBL was probably the most commendable thing he's done. Every other decision was a day late and a dollar short in my opinion. We can't afford for him to be a day late and a dollar short with the economy.

The sad part of all of this is that even when we don't want to spend money on something he does it anyway. He has committed us to so much foreign aid already, that we can't pay for any time soon. He's out there giving away some more right now. Stop already!

We have been told that many of our programs have vastly been outdated by other current programs. Our representatives get hung up on one project and they won't let go or try to determine if private funding could be better. In a report that was on the news, they mentioned how many duplicate programs are out there. The old one is kept even though the new one is in place and active. That's double spending in my book.

How about the hammers that we paid hundreds of dollars for or the programs to entertain the detainee's in our jails? Are you kidding me? They actually wanted to provide for the entertainment of illegal aliens. Give me a break.

Give me the list of programs and how much is spent on them. I'll be happy to cut some spending. It may take me a little longer, but I would make a significant amount of cuts. The lizard would have to learn to live somewhere else.

One of the first changes I would be making, after that, is that every Senator and House Representative would have to pay for their own health insurance and contribute to their own pensions. They would probably fight a lot harder if they were under our same plans. Their salaries are pretty hefty anyhow and how many days do they work for it? Hmm. When you get elected it's for a term not a lifetime! There are too many lifers in there. We need new blood at least every four years. I think they begin to be much too comfortable and forget what they were elected to do.

Probably they all started out with good intentions,

but somewhere along the line those good intentions fall by the wayside. Then it's who can get the most time in the political arena. How long can they stay in? I'm so sick of all the corruption and scandals we have to hear about.

First and foremost, the budget crisis should be the number one issue right now. The most obvious thing to do is balance the budget. That's a given. No one can function without a budget. How would you know how much you can spend?

Who can live like this? It's not an endless supply that we're talking about. When you reach your limit on your personal credit card, the card gets taken away and you have to pay it back. You quit spending or you go bankrupt. My point exactly.

So when do we get our budget for 2012? When does the spending end? When will all the bickering stop and the cuts begin? I certainly hope it starts soon.

Then there's the talk about a new world currency. We weren't invited to one of the meetings with Brazil, Russia, India and China. That's the meeting where they were discussing substituting the dollar for the world currency. As you know, when oil is bought, for instance, it is priced in US dollars. Almost everything is dependent on the US dollar. The world is looking at us in a different way now. Not as the world power but as a declining nation with many money woes. Does Obama think that by going to Ireland, Europe, and all these other countries we have promised money to that it will change their minds about our standing? Not a chance. Just listen to the news on BBC some time. That's an eye opener.

If we can come to an agreement on the spending our government should do, I think we may have a chance to survive. Everyone knows our current course of runaway spending is unsustainable. We can't keep doing it. We won't even be able to pay the interest due. You don't think the Federal Reserve is going to forgive our debts do you? Unlike Obama who "forgave" Libya's debts to us. Geez…what is he smoking? What are they all smoking? Do we ever get paid back?

Have you ever listened to one of Obama's speeches and then tried to figure out if he really said anything? I could give those speeches as effectively. Never any details spoken and only generalities are given and for that he needs a teleprompter? It's all the same old rhetorical garbage with no content.

The only speech he ever made that really mattered was about the death of UBL. That's the one I really thought was worthy. It looks as though they would have briefed each other a little better before they spoke about it though. The stories changed daily.

There I go again off on a tear. Wouldn't you like to be a fly on the wall in one of those private meetings of the "Super Committee?" I would. I'd like to know if they are really listening to what they are proposing for solutions or if they are playing Monopoly with the funds of America. Hey, there is no "free pass". These men were appointed by Obama and our Congress but, he doesn't listen. What did he appoint them for if he wasn't going to take any advice? Was it just to make himself look good, you know, as if he was deeply concerned?

Do you wonder what the rest of the world really discusses behind our backs? I know from watching World News that we aren't respected any more. If you watch newscasts from the Middle East and Northern Africa you see the hate they have for the US. They sure take our handouts though. Just maybe we should cut ALL foreign aid for now. Don't you just wonder how long it would take for them to be knocking on our door? You certainly can't blame them when we push money in their faces.

Let's talk about the Entitlement programs that

we have. Social Security is going broke. This is a given. Personally, I couldn't make it without my $733 per month. It would be a real hardship. Though the age of retirement is not realistic any more. People are out-living their funds not only because of inflation, but they are living longer. I flip houses when I can and had a part time job to make ends meet. My skills happen to be labor oriented not white collar skills. How much longer can I keep that up? I don't know. I'm 65 years old.

Paul Ryan is right with respect to people already on Social Security. How can you pull the rug out from under someone my age at this point? And his plan doesn't do that. I don't have so many years left or skills to be able to replace my Social Security. It's something that you plan for early in life. Ryan's plan addresses the younger people who do have a chance to plan differently. They have the time to prepare and save.

I have to share a comment my kids made the other day. We were talking about the national debt, who isn't, and my daughter-in-law said they know they can never retire. They know they will work their entire lives.

How sad that's what legacy we are leaving them. There are a lot of people out there in the same boat. On top of that, we are burdening them with huge bills from the current administration. Hey, he can't blame Bush now, not after three years.

Social Security is not the biggest expense that we have. Medicare is and we all know this, too. The ObamaCare program is not working either. When Social Security was removed from its private trust and into the national budget, that was a major mistake. The more money available to rob, the more they rob.

When I saw the size of the Bill and heard all the complaints about how no one has had time to study it, I knew we were being had again. Come on, can't you just do something without a trillion earmarks and favorite pet programs attached? Do you have to buy your votes on our backs? Wouldn't it have been much cheaper to pay for the "uninsurable's" insurance under a specially designed program for them? Lord knows you think of programs to save lizards and study the mating habits of some obscure animal. Couldn't you have set aside some program for that?

Thanks a lot, Obama, my insurance deductible went up to $3500 per year. And that was all because of the fear you have caused that small businessman. Thanks a lot. I didn't need that kind of help.

The insurance companies are big business.

Everything in the medical field is too expensive. You can't really blame the doctors because they are usually part of a group and they are run as a business. They are told how many patients they must see a day and what they should be doing in their practice. We are just a number any more. So many doctors are turning away from the normal practice of medicine because of all the hassle they have from ObamaCare. I do empathize with them.

You've heard of the death panels haven't you? It's big business again telling the doctor's how or if they should treat us or not from some actuary chart they look at to see if you are or you aren't "worth" saving or treating. I guess I'll be placed on that list of don't treat any further at some point. Whoopee! Again, thanks a lot.

Don't you just love the advertisement on tv that shows Granny being dumped over the mountain? Or the one where the old guy is mowing the lawn while pushing his walker? The Democrats are responsible for these ads and they aren't true references to the Ryan Plan. We are not being deserted or abandoned by his plan. Read the darn thing.

What exactly has Obama's Plan done for us but cost us so much more and place a burden on all

50

businesses? Do you recall hearing the news blog about how a national burger chain was having to change their whole health program. They had to lay off people so they could pay for the changes from Obama Care?

Our system has flaws but not so bad that we couldn't tweak it and come up with something better than ObamaCare.

Now to get to the true problem with our budget is Medicaid. I'm not talking about the little old lady who has no family, she's sick, has no means of support. I'm talking about the alcoholic who uses his money to get more booze and has worked the system for years. I'm talking about the gal who gets knocked up and then has four more kids who works the system. I'm talking about the illegals who somehow manage to get in the system and stay there. I'm talking about the druggies that work it. I'm talking about the alcoholics that rape the system for booze with no intention to get a job.

Now I sound like I hate the down and trodden group. Nope. Not so. If my Mother hadn't had help, Mom was blind and in a wheelchair, I wouldn't have a dime left. Right before she died I got her help from Medicaid. Thank you for that one. Up until then I paid for her ear cleanings, hearing aids, pedicures because she was diabetic, her clothes, and anything else that she needed to get. It was a huge strain on my already over-burdened budget. I'm not the least bit sorry I did it though. You don't abandon someone just because they get old. They aren't like an old pair of shoes you throw out when they show wear and tear.

And you know, I think anyone can be down on their luck at times. Like the poor homeless who are making tent camps in our woods outside of town, the so-called shanty towns. They need help, but not the kind they are getting. They need a roof over their head, some counseling, and a chance to work somewhere doing something that makes them feel worthy again. If every church took on four homeless people and helped them out, the problem would have a long way of creating productive people and getting them off our system. What a worthy project that would be. We sure have enough abandoned homes to help provide housing. And, they would be doing us a favor to do the physical upkeep of the houses, too.

It is sad to see some young gal who got raped or abused or knocked up from some trick she just turned. These women need help. They need counseling, a place to live, and a job. Sometimes there seems like there's the opinion of some young girls that there is no other way out but to turn tricks. We shouldn't judge them too harshly. Would you blame the young girl who was being abused by a step-father or mother's boy-friend or her own father for running away? Thank God I had a loving caring Mother and Father. I feel sorry for those who didn't.

How about the father who just got laid off because of spending cuts? He's over-trained and overqualified for most jobs or under-trained and not qualified for any job. Sure, he probably has savings to last for a little while, but when that runs out what about him? Or he has none at all. Either scenario is heart wrenching.

What about the single Mom out there trying to find a job? She has to find someone to sit with her kids to even be able to go out looking for employment. By the time the day care is paid, if she does find work, there's no money left for food and clothes or a place to live.

Most of the people on welfare are honest folks just trying to make it to the next day. But, there are some who have been on unemployment draws for way longer than should be allowed. Ninety-nine weeks is too long. I actually know of a few people who have remarked that they will wait until their checks run out and then go look for a job. In this case, they should be cut off after a six month period and re-evaluated.

There is something called the Labor Force here where if you show up on time, you get a chance for employment for the day. Whoever hires you pays the Labor Force and you get paid that same day in cash. It's minimum wage, but if you're a healthy body you can get work. I think most cities have this.

I truly don't believe that people would rather sit around collecting checks they haven't earned than be gainfully employed and have money to be able to make their lives better and easier. The social aspect of being out there in the work force is therapeutic by itself. Humans mostly are social animals. We generally like to be around other people. I think we have more pride than that, too. There are some though that just want to try the system.

How about the guy who just won $2,000,000 in a lottery and is on food stamps? His reply when he was questioned was that he wasn't feeling guilty about it at all. He actually had made a call and verified that he could still get food stamps.

Where's this man's pride? Shame on him and shame on a system that lets him get away with it. He cleared $850,000 out of that deal. Poor guy! I guess if he hadn't been on food stamps he never would have been able to buy that lottery ticket. Hmm.

What's the answer to all this? I'm certainly not educated well enough and not privy to the insider information I would need to solve the problems, but I do have a few suggestions as to how I would tackle the deficits of our country. I have always had a really hard time of seeing the gray areas. I'm pretty cut and dry but that seems to be working for me.

The approach I would take to our budget woes would be pretty direct. These things are what I would do immediately after we balance the budget. That would be a given.

First, all foreign aid would be suspended and most of our troops would be withdrawn. This would be for a period of six months. After that, the promise of giving aid would be revisited and re-evaluated. We would have to have a clear goal, a plan for re-entry and an exit plan, and funds in place with a budget limit. Other countries would have to be made to understand that we have to pull back for now, but it may be only temporary. They would then see who their "friends" really are.

Secondly, our troops would be brought home and placed on our Southern borders where they all desperately needed. They would be armed and dangerous. Arrests and deportations would be made in conjunction with the Mexican government. All the underground tunnels, everyone has known about for years, would be blown up and sealed.

They would have the right to look at papers to see if there are any. If there are no legal papers then they should be asked to either return with them, sent back, then get in line to start a legal immigration into the States. More offices would be provided for this process. This process would come at a price. That price would be enlisting in the service or to be placed in employment to be taught a skill along with a loan to be paid back to our government for this privilege. That means more jobs. If we eliminate half of our empty non-productive programs we could probably fund this quiet handily. How about having the illegals that have criminal backgrounds work on "chain gangs" to repair our infrastructure? They would receive no pay for this.

Thirdly, every member of Congress would have their salaries reviewed and cut by 25% right off the top. They would be paying for their own insurance and lifetime pensions would be ended. They would get a severance pay after their term is up. I'm not talking about a huge funding. I'm talking about a two week severance pay like everybody else gets. These terms are not meant to be lifetime jobs. There comes a point when your mind is not quite as sharp as it could be.

We all know some elected members who qualify for "retirement". Some of the things that come out of their mouths are incredible sometimes. You wonder how they could possibly make an educated decision on any issues. They usually don't judging from some of the programs that have been passed.

Shouldn't our Congressional seats be represented year round? A two week vacation should be permitted while they are in office. Who do you think pays for their vacations? Actually, a lot of what they do could be done from computers, conference calls, and by phone.

Fourth in line would be the Entitlements. I would keep people already enrolled in Social Security and the ones coming into the system in ten years or less in the current program guidelines. Anyone fifty five years or younger would be eligible to draw half of their contributions at age sixty five and their full retirement contribution at seventy. Or they could opt out of the entire program and retrieve twenty five percent of their contributions in the form of monthly payments calculated on the amount of their contribution to date with the term of the payment figured on that amount.

There are plenty of Americans who really don't need Social Security. They could elect not to collect it and receive in return some sort of tax credit. There are citizens whose income should not necessitate their being in the program anyway. There would have to be a limit of measured income set to eliminate them. Does Warren Buffett or Donald Trump need Social Security? I think not and they would probably be willing not to take advantage of the program.

The same would be true of Medicare. Those who could afford to purchase our own private insurance should do just that and opt out of Medicare. Most of us are paying for a private supplementary program anyhow. Also, the deductible would have to adjust to probably seventy five per cent coverage.

It would definitely call for a re-structuring of how our insurance is charged now. It's getting changed anyway by ObamaCare. The cost of prescriptions is way out of hand. How many times have you heard a report where a huge premium is paid for a pill that costs forty cents to make? And, we are an over-medicated society, in most instances. The amount of pills my parents were on was mind boggling.

I had a condition called Fibromyalgia for fifteen years. They think that Fibromyalgia is , they think, caused by incorrect signals sent from the brain and misinterpreted by it only to send a message of pain to the body. I was given about ten pills to take and was wiped out most of the time. The pain associated with it was horrendous. I'm not a whiner. I hated taking all those medications.

Funny thing, it went completely away the day I finally broke up with the ex. That and the fact that I simply quit taking all the pills cold turkey. Heaven forbid, I'm not suggesting that anyone do that. Talk to your physician. My point is that I was prescribed too many pills.

Drug companies often give trips away or favors to the doctors for prescribing their particular product. That should not be allowed under any circumstances. You should be prescribed medication because you need it to function not because it's the latest thing or there's a big promotion going on with a gift attached.

You can't blame the doctor wholly either. Maybe the latest greatest does work better. I have yet to visit my doctor where there isn't a drug rep sitting there in the waiting room with their bag full of new scripts. I hate that, especially when I have already been sitting there waiting for thirty minutes or so.

Most of the time a simple blood test is the marker for whether we need something to be prescribed or not. The LDL is high or maybe triglycerides are off, maybe hormones or vitamins. Anyone can get their blood pressure taken with the machines at local drug stores. It's free. I do mine every week when I get groceries. If my pressure is high I would call my doctor and discuss it with him. Anyone with more severe problems would still have to go see his primary physician more often anyway.

If you have an emergency, the doctor's office tells you to go to the emergency room or a walk-in clinic. That's a totally different scenario. The emergency room is not a revolving door though. It's not to be over used for just any problem. It definitely gets abused. I have witnessed that first hand. My first job was in an emergency room. Believe me, it was an abused facility.

Then there's Medicaid. Anyone sixty five or older that is on Medicaid should be re-evaluated to make sure they are being taken care of properly. I think you have to fill out the paperwork every year for that and I think at that age it would be sufficient to be checked yearly.

How about the young girl or single Mom? First off, the young girl who got pregnant out of wedlock needs to be schooled if under eighteen and assigned a family, a sponsor, big sister maybe. I'm sure the study of how many nails are in some bridge and how long will it be before they keep from rusting might be an important program to sponsor, but our young girls need it much worse than the nails. Foster homes are available and many are privately financed.

The single Mom who isn't receiving any type of support from the Father of the child who has been through the legal system to get it and doesn't receive payments should be helped out and the situation re-visited in one year, also.

She should be networked with other single moms in the area so that children could be watched together in a sort of babysitting pool. That's how we did it when we needed day care. None of us could afford to leave the house otherwise. It worked great. It helped our budgets immensely.

The alcoholics or drug users must be checked every three months. I mean physically checked for drugs and alcohol usage. They must attend counseling and must be making an effort to become drug free and gainfully employed. Community hours should be assigned at that time, too. Idle hands in a drug user's life or an alcoholic's life are the worst thing that could happen. After six months of counseling, if the effort is not being put forward then they must be dropped from the system that is enabling them. At that point, you probably won't change them. Hopefully, someone will be able to reach them and persuade them to change themselves. They have to want it.

Everywhere I go there is an opportunity to create jobs for our populace. I understand why businesses have scaled back. We all know it's because of our economy. But, at some juncture in our measly little lives, we have to make some sacrifices for the good of America.

We all have to help each other out. I am having my pool cleaned every month because the kid who cleans it really needs his job. He just bought a house for $58,000 and was so proud of it. Believe me, I am not lazy. I used to do my own pool cleaning. Every week he comes to work, I look at him and listen to how happy his kid is to have a back yard to play in now. I just can't let him go.  That doesn't sound like much, but it is a lot for my budget. I bought this house to flip in a year or two, hopefully at a small profit.

I paid $500 extra to have the plantation shutters I put in this house because they were not made in China. They are made in the good ole USA. I would do that every chance I can if I can afford it. Just think what it would mean if we all pitched in just a little. Those efforts that make a difference. They do add up.

The unemployment checks should stop and be re-visited after six months. The applications should be reviewed and examined as to why they didn't get that particular job. Perhaps their aspirations are very unrealistic. Dishwashing may not be a luxurious job or flipping burgers in the local fast food joint may not be what your really want to do for a lifetime, but it helps pay the bills. There are courses that can be taken very reasonably at the local Vocational Technical Schools that give you the opportunity to learn a skill if you don't have one. You have to be assertive and take the initiative on your own. It isn't going to fall into your lap. Our financial system can't afford to carry you. Usually you become some sort of apprentice after that, but many jobs allow you the opportunity to have your own business.

If there has been no effort to try to find a job then you have to decide whether the applicant has truly made an effort and if you feel you are allowing them to sit at home and be a couch potato. Just maybe they would try a little harder. There are jobs out there but you have to become inventive. There are many good programs and grants available that are wonderful sources to improve yourself.

Fifth in line would be all the vast programs in our system that are duplicate programs. Many of these programs happen because someone wants a favor and will guarantee a vote. We have all heard about those people. When a new program is introduced to improve on the older one, the older one stays in place, too, thereby doubling the expense.

There are, also, many programs that could be privately funded just fine. I think that the Planned Parenthood might be one of those. I'm pro-life myself, but programs like this could be privately funded. Women can get Pap Smears without having to go to Planned Parenthood. Families should handle their unwed, under age, pregnant children as they see fit. That's where parenting comes into the picture. It should be a private concern.

I would like to know how many programs could be sent back out for private funding. Studies of the mating calls of a certain type of whale should be in a marine environment and privately funded.

Out-of-date programs that serve no purpose except to take funding from the government have to stop. You know, those earmark projects that seem to slide through in a bill. There are many thousands of those kind of projects.

Where is the store that sells hammers for $200 a

piece? Are they imported from some other country? Knowing our government they probably are. These kind of expenses have to have some oversight.

Who knows better how much should be budgeted for our towns than the City Planners and the Mayor? Then why are we not able to pay our bills? Oh yea, some of that fault comes from the big fat pensions that our retired government workers get. Boy, did that get out of hand. We can't afford it guys. This, too, will have to change.

That brings us back to Unions, too. Teachers make a pretty fair living. I don't think they should not be able to be replaced and tenure should not enter into it at all. There are good teachers and bad teachers. They have learned to work the system, too. Honestly, if I were a teacher I probably would have, too. Legally, we permit it to happen. Change is coming. Florida is a right to work state, but that doesn't mean the right to "work the system" state. Let's take a good look at what unions should offer and overturn some of those powers that are given to the Union bosses, many times with the laborers unaware of what they have used the dues for.

Sixth, would be to encourage the goal of entre-preneurship. Somehow we have forgotten how to be practical about most issues. We do the easy thing rather than the hard one. Our inventiveness has become stifled and almost non-existent except where working the system is involved. We all do it to some extent.

One big reason for the lack of incentives for the entrepreneur is our beloved EPA. Good grief, I want to help save our planet, too, but haven't we gone way overboard on that, too?

We would be self efficient if we could get the EPA to lighten up some. Way too many rules and regulations. Then there are the endless studies that have to be done when an infraction is found.

Drilling was halted because some little lizard wants to live there. Are you kidding me? Move the dang lizard to another area. Progress has come to complete halt due to some lizard. Believe me, he'll learn to adjust. That's craziness. Let us drill baby drill!

I don't hate the EPA. I do think we have to consider the good of the majority though. How about reducing the number of different gases we make? Could you lighten up on that a little?

Where were you when Chinese drywall came into

our ports and ruined literally thousands and thousands of homes? Hmm. Must have been out looking for that lizard that day.

How about spending some time really trying to promote new energy for us without putting so dang many rules that it can't be made profitable? You are stunting our growth and progress.

We have many brilliant people, inventors, out there, but somehow their projects get hung up in paperwork. Let them invent for gosh sakes. Give them some tax breaks and less controls, a little levity.

I can't remember ever having a problem when I was growing up with my environment. We all just sort of took it upon ourselves to do the right thing. We didn't dump chemicals in the ground. We used some DDT for spraying bugs and we had our own mixtures of organic stuff that worked. None of my friends have three eyes or four arms. That's not really fair, I guess, just because we were in an area that didn't have big factories. We had horse farms and oranges and cattle.

Love Canal is still a wasteland. That's still where the EPA should be watching, not the small farmer who wants to grow something. The EPA has a place in situations regarding hazardous wastes.

The big oil spill was due to people not doing the maintenance and service checks properly. The other wells are doing their due diligence now so why aren't we drilling?

Cuba has just announced they are drilling at the edge of our border off the coast of Florida. Wouldn't it be more prudent to do our own drilling and this way we can keep an eye on them better? I just don't get it.

The seventh thing I would do is get rid of the huge fleets of vehicles that our government has in use.  Are they driving electric cars? Are the planes Lear jets or jumbo jets? Obama flies all over the place all the time. Couldn't he save a little gas himself? What happened to video conference calls? I think he should be setting an example for all of us.

Of course, the story just broke that one of those "green" projects is supplying the jet fuel and charging around $15.00 per gallon. No crony capitalism there!

I just wonder if there is a gas pump that does nothing but fill up the vehicles for our government employees. I'll bet there is. Of course there is. Guess who pays for that in the long run? Must be nice to have your gas paid for especially at the prices we pay today.

The eighth thing I would do is do away with the Federal Reserve. We owe them a ton of money already. Why should the Federal Reserve have the say so on what the interest rates should be? Who gave them that power? Our banking and financial systems are under their thumb.

Everything they do effects the Stock Markets. Why do we need the Federal Reserve at all? Why are they so secretive? What would happen if we got rid of them?

I'm not sure I understand how it all works. I know that when our dollar was backed by gold, we stored it in Fort Knox. I saw a documentary that said they really don't believe there is any gold in Fort Knox. That we have spent it all. Ok. If we have spent it then did we pay it to the Federal Reserve to keep our debt down?

I saw another documentary that said the Federal Reserve doesn't have any gold either. Then where is the gold? It wasn't all ours. We stored gold for other countries. Where's their gold? Is it in the World Bank? I don't get it. Doesn't the US Mint get their gold from the Treasury to make gold coins? Where did that gold come from for the coins? It sounds like everything goes in a big circle. Oh, in that same documentary, they mentioned that there is no money there. That it's

69

all digitally stored and that's why when we need money they print more. Boy, does this make sense to you? Something is just not right.

If supposedly, the Federal Reserve was started by five world bankers and they owned a quarter of the world's wealth. Then in the early 1900's when JP Morgan bailed us out of debt, is it at that point that the gold that backed our dollar went into the Federal Reserve? I know the second time we needed money, JP Morgan said no. Did we borrow from the Fed itself? Is that when all this mess got started?

It's my understanding that if we could get rid of the Reserve, we will still owe our debt to them unless they sell our debt to someone else. Just how many vacation homes and Lear jets can you own? What would they do if we defaulted on our debt to them? Go on another vacation probably. They have more money than any of us can fathom.

This is scary. How would you like to have to learn to speak Russian or Chinese? Not a comfortable feeling to me.

The ninth part of this plan would be to make an across the board, flat rate tax for everyone. The IRS could be eliminated totally. This is probably the most fair way to do it.

There are so many loopholes in the tax codes for the people who can afford the tax attorneys to interpret those laws, that the average person doesn't stand a chance. There would be just a few tax credits allowed. There would have to be a rate for businesses and for individuals. Our corporate rates are the highest in the World. That discourages growth inAmerica for sure. Those loopholes have to be redefined, too, for big business. I think it's awful when a company gets bailed out then pays zero taxes. Give me a break.

I heard today on Fox News that the government paid out huge sums to companies that had delinquent taxes. Are you serious? Just try not paying your taxes and see what happens. I hope they are checking that loophole, too.

The final thing I would do is make the banks do a readjustment for the homeowners with homes under water. I think it is absurd that homeowners are sitting in their homes not making any attempt to pay anything. That's not right. No one forced the owners to borrow so much on the homes.

I got our residence in a divorce settlement. He got two other homes. Because I had to try to take him

back to court because of another issue, I had to get a
mortgage on the home I had gotten in the settlement.
After two and a half years, I finally got the chance to
have a mediation. The mediation was a matter of
principle for me. I knew he had protected everything
else and hidden it from me. I got very little in the
mediated settlement. The value of the home was
dropping like a lead balloon. The payments were high.
I bit the bullet, sold the home, and had to come up with
$35,000 out of my pocket to pay the mortgage off.

The people who bought the house paid $25,000 and
I paid $35,000. It made me sick to do it but I could not
afford to carry the mortgage. I could have lived in it for
probably two years and not paid a dime to live there
other than utilities. Nobody forced me to borrow so
much money. I did not want to short sale it or have a
foreclosure against me. I was brought up to pay my
way and pay back what I borrow. It was a matter of
pride to me. I have worked extremely hard to build my
credit rating.

I realize there are circumstances beyond anyone's
control. But why not make half a payment? Make some
attempt to pay your debt back. I soon saw that everyone was playing the system there, too. In Florida it
was taking two years to even get through a foreclosure. They gave it a name, too. They called it

strategic foreclosure. Many people did it because they could get away with it. I'm glad I did the honorable thing. Another reason I say why not pay something is, also, a personal one.

In this same divorce settlement, I was talked into taking first mortgages that we owned from having financed builders in the area. Three months after the divorce the mortgages fell apart and I received no more payments. I receive, as of January this year, about $345 a month for just under a million dollars worth of mortgages I hold. That million dollars worth of mortgages is probably worth a couple hundred thousand at best. I would have given anything if a partial payment had been made. I have spent a fortune on carrying these properties. I have had to pay many attorneys to help form LLCs for the lots in developments, back taxes, current taxes, code enforcement fees because they weren't keeping them cleared either. Boy, would I have really appreciated a token gesture. I would have gladly renegotiated the loans if I could find them to talk to them about it.

Our banks down here were actually happy to have homeowners remain in in these fore-closures because, in Florida, the occupied homes were at least somewhat taken care of and the air conditioning run. That helped keep vandals out and mildew down. Our courts were so loaded down with foreclosures that they did the rocket foreclosures. Sometimes they were not done with due care. A lot of law suits sprang out of that.

If the loans were even extended to forty years, that might make enough difference in payments that some people could stay and keep their homes. You can't expect to live free. You have to live somewhere. The rates are so low, it's time to refinance or re-negotiate the loans. This would at least get the foreclosure count down and the banks would clean up their books.

I'm sure doing just these things would make a huge difference in our national debt. Washington has to go on a diet! It's not fun getting up every day to hear the news anymore. The first thing you hear is "America, we're broke" and the last thing you hear is how we have given billions of dollars away again.

Obviously, the plan I have presented is not going to "fix" our economy. The suggestions are just that. Suggestions.

We all know this has got to change! I don't want to learn Mandarin or Russian or Farsi.

Chapter Five

## IN GOD WE TRUST!

**O**ops, I guess I'm not allowed to say that anymore in front of anyone. The heck with that. Have we totally forgotten why we came over in the first place? Wasn't it basically for having freedom of religion? God was an integral part of our life and our pursuit of happiness.

Our founding fathers believed in God. Just read the Constitution if you don't believe me. I understand what freedom of religion means quite well. Did they mean for it to be removed from everything we have known to honor since then?

Let me ask you, when you were in school, did you ever have a problem with someone not respecting the flag, not saluting it, or not saying the Pledge of Allegiance or singing the National Anthem? My class was full of all sorts of different ethnic backgrounds, but no one ever complained. Where have we gone wrong?

I believe everyone has a right to worship any religion they want to practice. But if they don't want to be a part of our country, then what are they doing here? I especially mean the flag burners and religious protesters. How dare they. Send them back to wherever they came from if they don't like our ways if they can't conduct themselves appropriately.  They can sit quietly while the flag is displayed and the Pledge said.

There are plenty of people who would give anything to live here. To have the rights and freedoms we have. Just look around the world now. The fighting and riots are for their desire to be a free country and have these rights. They may say they hate us, but they are fighting to have the same freedoms we do. They must not hate us that much.

We existed for many years together with people from all around the world with all sorts of cultural differences. They could live and worship as they pleased. So why is it that now God has become such an issue? Why is He so offensive to so many people now? Now one of our football players is being crucified for showing his love for his God. Please, at least he is a young man you can look up to instead of some of the other dog-fighting, womanizing, abusive players.

If we go to visit a foreign country, wouldn't you respect their country's flags and buildings and their culture? Would you ever think of going to a foreign country and burning their flag? Or asking them to remove something in your hotel because it insults you? Of course not. So who is it that is doing all this complaining? Is this an organized effort to cause problems all over the US? Makes you wonder what's really happening here.

Recently I received an email that claimed in the near future our population would be predominantly Muslim. That we were becoming more and more Muslim all the time. What? Huh? Am I missing something or is this really happening? I don't look good in black. I definitely wouldn't like to practice Sharia Law and wear a one of those hot black outfits. I'm a Southern girl. I can shoot what I aim to hit. I still enjoy going barefoot and wearing jeans. Sharia is not my bag! Not going to happen if I can help it.

I do not have a problem with anyone worshipping chickens or cows or anything as long as they don't impose their customs and practices on me. As long as they don't dishonor what we have established as our way of life, I don't have an issue. And will you leave my country, flag, the Constitution, and the Pledge of Allegiance alone please.

Have you seen this email yet? This is quoted as it was sent to me:

Australia says NO - Second Time she has done this !

AMAZING You must read it !!!! She's done it again.. She sure isn't backing down on her hard line stance and one has to appreciate her belief in the rights of her native countrymen. A breath of fresh air to see someone lead. I wish some leaders would step up in Canada & USA & UK. Australian Prime Minister does it again!! This woman should be appointed Queen of the World.. truer words have never been spoken. It took a lot of courage for this woman to speak what she had to say for the world to hear. The retribution could be phenomenal, but at least she was willing to take a stand on her and Australia 's beliefs. The whole world needs a leader like this! Prime Minister Julia Gillard - Australia

Muslims who want to live under Islamic Sharia law were told on Wednesday to get out of Australia, as the government targeted radicals in a bid to head off potential terror attacks..

Separately, Gillard angered some Australian Muslims on Wednesday by saying she supported spy agencies monitoring the nation's mosques.

Quote:

'IMMIGRANTS, NOT AUSTRALIANS, MUST ADAPT.. Take It Or Leave It. I am tired of this nation worrying about whether we are offending some individual or their culture. Since the terrorist attacks on Bali , we have experienced a surge in patriotism by the majority of Australians. ' 'This culture has been developed over two centuries of struggles, trials and victories by millions of men and women who have sought freedom' 'We speak mainly ENGLISH, not  Spanish, Lebanese,

Arabic, Chinese, Japanese, Russian, or any other language. Therefore, if you wish to become part of our society . Learn the language!'

'Most Australians believe in God. This is not some Christian, right wing, political push, but a fact, because Christian men and women, on Christian principles, founded this nation, and this is clearly documented It is certainly appropriate to display it on the walls of our schools. If God offends you, then I suggest you consider another part of the world as your new home, because God is part of our culture.'

'We will accept your beliefs, and will not question why - all we ask is that you accept ours, and live in harmony and peaceful enjoyment with us.'

'This is OUR COUNTRY, OUR LAND, and OUR LIFESTYLE, and we will allow you every opportunity to enjoy all this. But once you are done complaining, whining, and griping about Our Flag, Our Pledge, Our Christian beliefs, or Our Way of Life, I highly encourage you take advantage of one other great Australian freedom, 'THE RIGHT TO LEAVE'.' 'If you aren't happy here then LEAVE.

We didn't force you to come here. You asked to be here. So accept the country YOU accepted.'
End of the quote.

Excuse me, but I thank you for that email. Amen! Someone has the guts to say it! Boy, do I wish we did. It would solve a multitude of problems. Do I need to say more?

That brings me to the issue of the Ground Zero controversy over building that temple. Why would there be any question or discussion about where the Center for Cultural Awareness or whatever the heck name they came up with even have been considered at all? What a slap in the face. Oh, I know they were radicals and terrorists, but how on earth did 9/11 happen?

One of the pilots was training in an airport twenty miles from here. This is a very small airport. Wouldn't you have been a little suspicious or at a little curious? I at least try to be aware of my own close surroundings. What a horrible day that was for all of us. It was the turning point in how we live our everyday lives now.

I wonder how long it will be before the inscriptions including the word "God" will have to be chiseled off all of our national monuments? Oh, geez, I probably shouldn't have even written that because some nut will latch onto that idea and go run with it. And they will probably try to sue Washington or our government. That's just how absurd things have gotten.

Did you see on the news yesterday where some serviceman was coming home and the town was honoring him with placing flags on the light poles and that caused a huge problem? It had to do with a ridiculous law that had been put on the books that said if the flags were hung on the poles, the electric company had to charge them a fee. Now this was a small town. The town's citizens raised over eight thousand dollars to pay the fee. Holy cow, it's way out of whack.

Have you visited your child's school rooms lately? Are the flags still up in their rooms? Have you checked out the books they are required to teach out of, too? Since when is it alright to teach that Marxism or Socialism is good and that democracy is not the way to live? Hello there. Believe me it is happening. How is it that these books are being approved? Who is behind all of that?

When we were in school learning world history, we were taught about Marxism and Socialism, but never was there any kind of suggestion that a democratic government was not what we all were living and fighting for every day. I went through the Cold War. We had many drills during my childhood in preparation for a possible nuclear attack. The Cuban Crisis was at my back door. All of us wouldn't have our government be anything but a democracy. When did this all change?

The internet has become a wonderful tool for our children, but that gets abused, too. How well are your kids being monitored on their school computers? What sites are they being instructed to visit? Who controls that?

We have all heard the news stories of the abuses from school children to other students. I realize it's hard to keep an eye on it, but some-one's not watching them closely enough. If they would just allow the volunteers back in the classrooms, that problem could be monitored much better.

What is all this bullying about, too? Since when don't you get sent to the principal's office immediately for that? Why is there so much antagonism from the students? Why is there so much hate and disrespect? Who's fault is that? Why are classrooms disruptive to the point the teacher can't teach? Are the teachers not in control? Are they afraid to say anything anymore for fear of reprisal from the students they correct? Wow. This is totally unacceptable.

What about the little kid that had a pistol in his backpack and he dropped it and it went off and hurt another child? Parents, I blame you for that. If you have weapons in your home, no matter how old your kids are, they should be locked up in a safe place. The children should be educated properly about what a weapon is there for and what the rules are to use to it.

I'm a Southern girl and, yes, before you ask, I hunted with my Dad when I was eight years old. I didn't carry a rifle until I was much older. In fact, I was made to take a Junior Riflemen's Course at eleven years of age to learn how to handle the gun properly, to learn the laws, and to learn to respect the power and damage that it could render. There was no foolishness associated with hunting with a rifle. When I participate in a shoot, I am thankful that I took this course. I'm not saying you have to go that far, but teach your kids to respect it. Lock the darn gun up so they can't get it.

Children are exposed every day to stories about the killings on our borders. The daily news is filled with graphic pictures of the wars and riots overseas. Take the time to explain why these riots and struggles are going on and what they are desperately trying to attain. Just maybe your kids will realize that the world wants what we have. They want freedom and rights. You have to make the kids feel hopeful and thankful for the rights and freedoms we enjoy. Our children have seen and heard nothing else but wars since they were born. We have to give them hope no matter what. Believe me, I know how hard it is to trust with the world the way it is now.

Do you think just maybe we are pushing our kids a

little too hard when it comes to acting their age? Babies aren't dressed in baby clothes anymore. They look as though they are trying out for some television commercial for the preppy kid look.

How about our teenagers? I swear some of them look like sluts walking in the classroom. Are you trying to encourage letting your kid get knocked up? Parents have to say no. Where's your right as a parent to limit the length of the skirt and the neckline of the shirt or tee? It's still there so use it. Why are the schools allowing some of this to go on when they see them coming into the classroom? For gosh sakes, give them time to mature. It's no wonder there's such a huge percentage of pregnancies in eleven year olds. Some thirteen year olds look like they are twenty.

I just love it when the guys walk in and there underpants are showing out the top of their jeans or trousers. The trousers are down around their knees. It's ok to wear hand me downs, but shouldn't they wear belts to hold their pants up? School is not a place to make a fashion statement. Way too much time is being spent on what they are wearing, or not wearing, instead of what they are learning.

Our children don't know how to write, spell, or use

correct English. They know how to protest and riot. They know how to work the system, too. It's no wonder they can't get jobs. They aren't qualified to write a resume. It's all about passing the state tests so the schools and teachers get rewarded. What a waste of good minds. How discouraging.

The average graduate wouldn't be able to make a budget or write a check. Of course, our Congressmen can't either so I shouldn't be too harsh about that. Our kids aren't prepared for the world out there. They are not being taught the skills to make it on their own. No wonder they end up in gangs, stealing and into drugs or prostitution.

We are all so busy trying to make ends meet that we are beginning to forget what parenting even means. Where are the kids who have chores to do when they get their homework done? Why are the grades going down along with the "respect" factor for their Mom and Dad? Kids don't respect their parents or their siblings anymore.

You don't have to be a religious fanatic to be a Christian or believe in God. You don't have to be in church on Sundays, but you do need to emphasize how God has an important role in our lives. I think we have gotten far away from that. What happened to the

Golden Rule? It's been morphed into "Do unto others before they do unto you". The Ten Commandments obviously aren't being practiced either. That's the family's fault. These rules are what form our character and give us boundaries and guidelines for everyday life.

We aren't nice to each other anymore. We have forgotten how to be considerate and caring for anyone else.

I don't care what faith you practice, as long as the rules and guidelines meld into a fair and just treatment of our fellow human beings. If they are so apparently opposite from the beliefs of our country, then why are you living here? Or practice them in private, but don't try to destroy our beliefs.

This just has to change. It's time.

## Chapter Six

## MY HOME IS MY CASTLE ?

**W**ell, it used to be. Being one of the biggest investments made by the majority of us, it was part of the American Dream. Everybody worked hard to be able to get out of that apartment and buy your dream house. You didn't even mind that you were going to owe thirty years. In fact, you had high hopes of burning that mortgage paper early because you were going to get it paid off sooner. Fat chances of that happening nowadays.

Everyone, especially here in Florida, is very familiar with the failing markets. Even in the beautiful resort areas I live in, the property values tanked. Not only did the housing sales drop off, but the seasonal rentals for our tourists bit the dust, too.

Greed had a lot to do with our housing problems. Greed on the part of the bankers, the investors, the house flippers, and homeowners out to make a killing. The stage was set for Ponzi schemes galore. And we had them. Flippers could make a killing without ever having to struggle to do it. Banks were very eager to loan money and encouraged you to push it to the limit. Banks sprung up all over the place. It used to be a local joke when a ground breaking occurred because usually it was for another bank. Many of them have closed and have since gone bankrupt themselves.

When you live in a Paradise it doesn't take much to entice buyers to the area. Lots and lots of building went on with huge projects springing up everywhere. Houses that were older were torn down and monster homes were built on the site where they had once stood. Real estate prices soared out of control. Then the bottom fell out. Payments were high and couldn't be kept current. Builders were dying on the vine. Projects came to a halt and the market was flooded with new homes and older builds.

Then we had the Chinese drywall problem. Entire neighborhoods were infected with this drywall. It turned your wiring black, ruined air conditioners and your appliances, pitted your pipes and fixtures, and some say gave off an odor. Health problems were reported, too. How this ever could have happened I will never ever understand.

The story came out where a huge freighter carrying the drywall was not let into port in a timely fashion. The drywall got wet and stayed that way for some time. Have you ever smelled mildew before? Of course, trying to buy the cheapest product available had its own part in all of it. It gave off some type of gas that affected everything. The Chinese don't have the same code requirements for making drywall like we do. That just added to the problems we already had.

You could watch the value of your home drop almost daily. It was very frustrating to have to sell a home. When I had to sell my home, there were so many foreclosures in my neighborhood that dragged my home's worth down that I didn't stand a chance to sell it for more. It cost me $35,000 to sell my home up and above all the normal costs. My credit is wonderful because I honored my responsibility to pay my debt. I knew I have to count on my credit being my word because of now being single. What if I needed to get a loan in the future? I was told that if you did a short sale your credit would go down at least 100 points immediately. I couldn't afford to let that happen.

I was fortunate to get out of it when I did. So many other people are stuck between a rock and a hard spot. They are the ones that needed help. Our banks were not loaning any money out. Refinancing was dang near impossible. Even when the stimulus money was out there the banks held onto their funds. It's still very difficult to get help from what I hear.

All these displaced families had to eventually move

out of the foreclosed homes so our rental market started to improve. Sales are picking up some, but most of them are short sales and foreclosures. Most of those are cash buyers, maybe speculators. There are some great deals out there if you have some money.

A lot of the condominiums went broke because they either didn't have them pre-sold or they didn't have enough in the complex to pay for the maintenance of the grounds, pools, and workers. You had to be real careful to make sure the budgets of the condos you were purchasing had a reserve or you had to pay more. Those assessments could be a lot. Plus the grounds might not get tended properly.

The oil spill in the Gulf caused more insecurity. Housing values fell a lot just from the fear of not having those beautiful beaches to go to or visit. Our whole economy depends on our visitors and retirees. If they weren't coming they weren't contributing to our local economy.

In our area there are a lot of second homes, too. Retirees bought them and rented them out until they were ready to retire. Suddenly the retirees weren't able to keep their places paid for either. First to go are second homes. Even our seasonal homes were not being rented. All of this contributed to the downfall.

The one redeeming factor that is helping us build back is that it is beautiful here. The housing costs are so reasonable compared to three or four years ago. You can buy a lot of house for your money compared to northern prices and you get wonderful weather with it. Year round sports and boating are our biggest draw. Hurricanes don't normally hit in our area so that usually doesn't deter someone from buying here.

It's almost like we are all having to start over again. Our previous biggest investment that was, also, our biggest asset isn't there. Many of us have become renters with slim chances of returning to real home ownership again. It takes many years to get over a short sale or foreclosure on your credit record. Actually, rentals are beginning to be in real demand because nobody can afford to buy even if they could qualify.

Many of my realtor friends say it will be four or five years before the market corrects and homes will have a decent return to value. I must say I agree. I hope it will be that soon. I really have my doubts.

How could anyone, in today's distressed economic condition, even want to consider taking the risk of home ownership? Every week we hear how the values have declined again. It will never get better until the economy stabilizes. I have my doubts about that happening, too. Taxes are going up, incomes coming down, inflation running the dollar down, all bad news.

The little house with the white picket fence is just a memory. I feel badly for our young couples who are just starting out. Home ownership for them will be a long way off for most.  I feel badly for the older couple who is trying to hang onto what they worked all the lives to have only to have to face the fact that rising costs are forcing them out. They can't even make a profit when they sell to go into that assisted living or nursing home. I feel badly for our children who see what must seem like the dream destroyed for them. How hard will they have to work to ever have a shot of owning a home?

The housing decline has severely hurt every small tradesman, too. Around here the larger home builders are under bidding the little guys for jobs so they can keep going until it picks up again. My Son is a state licensed electrician with his own company. He has had many of his fellow competitors go bankrupt because of the lack of jobs. It's a tough world out there. He had to let his employees go and felt really bad about it. He carried them for a while, but with two kids himself, he couldn't continue to do that and feed his family, too. Thank goodness, things are picking up a little. Lots of people are trying to fix up the home they are in if for no other reason than to put it on the market for sale.

Some of the neighboring cities were built with lots of land between the individual developments. Pipes were run and sewage and water were set in place. The main problem was that there were so few homes being built and sold the city couldn't afford to keep the utilities going. The costs to run all this piping and roadways far exceeded what they were making in revenues.

It's all the domino effect or the trickle down effect. One thing defaults then another and another because of that one. It's endless. The one good result was that you could buy a home there dirt cheap. Not a good trade-off. This just has to change.

Chapter Seven

## YOU CAN TAKE MY WORD FOR IT!

Yes, you can.  My word has always been good. If you ask me what one word I would use to describe what people think about me it would be integrity. I have great integrity. If I say I'm going to do it, you can bet your life on it. That's the way I was brought up. Dad would say you are only as good as your word and he meant it. What has happened to the world's integrity?

Every week we read about or hear a story about another celebrity or politician who is being prosecuted or denounced because they have broken their vows or their word. It's a universal problem, too. Look at the current head of the IMF who was accused of raping the maid. Tiger Woods and the Terminator and our Congress-men have filled the news with infidelity. Why do you bother to make these promises if you know you aren't going to keep them? Why get married at all? What's wrong with a society that has people we are supposed to be able to look up to breaking their word? Where are the morals and code of ethics for them?

Just today, the Fox News Channel, reported a survey about how people felt the morals of this country were rated as to the degree of morality. It didn't surprise me that about 67% of them said they felt the morals of our country were very poor. What a sad commentary.

After my divorce, one day when the ex was coming to the house to pick up something, I said  this t him. I said "Every night when I put my head down on my pillow, I know I have never cheated on anyone, intentionally hurt anyone, or broken a vow or promise that I have made. You can't do that and I feel sorry for you." He didn't know what to say. What a shame to have to treat someone you had been with almost forty years like that. It's been years since I have talked to him and will probably be many more to come.

I know one thing for sure and that is that there is no way we can possibly count on our government to tell the truth. You hear one story break and then shortly after that a totally different scenario. Look at what happened with the death of Bin Laden and that announcement. Can you believe all the different stories we got on that one?

Look what recently happened to Netanyahu. The speech that was made by Obama before he left on this last jaunt to Europe clearly stated that he felt the 1967 borders were going to have to go back into effect for Israel. The next minute Netanyahu announced those borders would be impossible to defend and that they would never agree to that. What an eloquent gentle man he seems to be. He very delicately stood his ground and put us in our place, but with great finesse.

Now the press is all over itself trying to backtrack Obama's statement about that. Obama went back on an agreement we had made in 2004 with Netanyahu. It made the word of the United States mean nothing. Obama's treatment of him was deplorable. He could have put off his tour until after Netanyahu spoke in front of Congress. What a slap in the face. And then to have the nerve to say how much their friendship means to us. Geez.

Our integrity as a nation is extremely important. We have got to make up a lot of lost ground from this administration. Our label as a super power is taking a back seat to a lot of other countries I never would have believed would even be considered as such.

Don't you love it when Obama is visiting with the European leaders and giving our money away like it was water, all the while giving them warnings about getting their budgets in order? Why the heck isn't he here working on our budget. Especially when his budget got voted down 100%. Talk about the kettle calling the pot black.

What kind of integrity was shown when the over two thousand page Health Care Bill was crammed hurriedly through? I thought I would croak when Pelosi says we will have to pass it to see what's in it. What kind of craziness is that? And look what a mess that darn bill has already caused.

It's not only rampant in our leadership and our Congress, but in our normal every day lives, too. How many times have you hired someone to do  something and later find out that they ripped you off because they didn't do it like they said they would? How many times has someone told you they were going to do some-thing and it never happens? Then they try to make you feel bad about it. There's a lot of that going on, too. It's so easy to tell the truth. I've done it so many times when I knew it would be so much easier to lie. My parents always said a lie will come back to bite you. They were right. It's so much better to tell the truth. It makes you feel good, honor-able. I could never lie growing up.

Just one time I would love to open up a newspaper and not have any stories about deceit and lies from people we all know. I really believe integrity gives you a strong backbone. It keeps you upright. The world sure needs to work on this one.

Putting integrity back in our government is almost an oxymoron. It shouldn't be, but it is. The words crooked and politician have become synonymous. What a shame. No wonder our world is in such a mess. No wonder we are falling apart as a nation. Our word doesn't mean anything anymore.

We have a story breaking now about one of our politicians who gave his friend a job and had prior knowledge of what was happening to Fannie Mae and Freddie Mac while he did it. Of course, he would have profited from this information. No surprises there. It figures we bail them out and then discover all the corruption involved.

Have you happened to see the ad where there is a man who resembles Paul Ryan and he is pushing an old lady off a cliff? That ad is so misrepresentative of what the program does. Why is it are they permitted to advertise bald faced lies? This, too, must change.

Chapter Eight

## WHAT TIME DO YOU GET OFF WORK?

Oh, that's right, you don't have a job. The jobs are disappearing right and left because small businesses can't afford to hire you. They are over-taxed and under appreciated. Their health care programs cost so much, thanks again Obama, that they are laying off people so they can pay for the ones they kept. Their cost for transportation is sky rocketing with the rising fuel costs which hits their pocket books. The cost of the products they use has risen dramatically. Who do you think pays more for that?

Corporate tax rates have run big factories overseas or across the borders. Of course, we just don't make anything anymore. Where's our Made in America tags? We all know what's happening there.

Unemployment checks are for too long as I stated earlier. Who wouldn't sit on their butts if they can make more by drawing from the government? That's our fault. We have become a nation of takers.

Why aren't we fixing our roads and infrastructures? Oh that's right, our cities are broke. When you have a gad zillion workers in unions and with government pensions you can't pay it all. Enough said about that.

I feel badly for our college graduates that are just coming into the job market now. It must be awfully depressing for them They have to compete with all the over-qualified laid off executives that are out there. Do you remember applying for your first job? What experience do you have? How could you have any experience if you just got out of school? It was tough back then. Can you imagine what it must be now?

Forget it if you're close to retirement age. There's not much out there. I'm too old for manual labor. You better pick the bridge you want to live under if you don't have lots of savings. You'll have to move the youngsters out of the way first. They are much better beggars, too. They can beg longer.

There are just too many of us looking at the same bridge or corner to work. I already have mine picked out, bridge that is. You wonder if the illegals were not here just how many more jobs would be out there.

They are everywhere you know. Funny thing. I once went to check a rehabber on a house I was financing. When I walked in the front door a whole bunch of people just disappeared. Now, I was only holding the mortgage on the place where I had loaned the funds for the redo, not the contractor. I asked the contractor where everybody went. He didn't have to answer me. I knew they were probably from the labor force. I told him he should be hiring locals that need the jobs and were naturalized. He told me all his workers were. Yea right. He ended up ripping me and the materials for the job off, too. I took a major loss on that one big time. Obviously, he was not a man of his word. He had no integrity, but he had enough materials to build himself a nice place.

Week after week we see the jobless rate usually going up. What is our government doing to help that? Is there something they could do? How about not sending every dime we have overseas for foreign aid to every country that says they need it? How about taking that money to hire workers to rebuild our roads and maybe strengthen our infrastructures? A billion dollars can hire a lot of people.

I had to laugh at a story John Stossel did recently. He had his make-up artist add a beard and dress him as though he was a beggar, John had a cardboard sign made he made up. One side was more the appeal to help because he is homeless. The other side said he liked beer and needed money for beer. Guess what happened? There was no difference between the amount he got using the different sides. He actually did quite well.

In that same story there was a young man and woman who dressed up as homeless people. They begged for money then walked back to what looked like a nice house two blocks away, changed into nice clothes and went shopping. She was interviewed about the happening. She didn't see anything wrong with it. What do you want to bet she was on unemployment and I will just bet that she had alreadyapplied for food stamps?

Our local paper ran a story about the shanty camps that were sprouting up in the North Port area. Many of these homeless people had tents. Of course, the fear is that they will set fire accidentally to the woods and burn the whole place down. It is private property I think. When the article was run, there was an out pouring of people who wanted to drop food off and clothing. You can't do that they said someone might get hurt. Since when is it a bad thing to want to help someone? What a shame.

It makes you feel good to do what you can to help. Neighbors helping neighbors, what's the harm in that? Why are we so distrusting of each other and so selfish? Everyone loves to feel good about helping someone less fortunate. That may be one of us someday.

What are we going to have to do to get jobs for everyone again? One thing, for sure, is to take care of our national spending and our national debt. Give us some sense of stability and some hope that we can turn this economy around. That's what is keeping our country down. Growth would explode if we balanced our budget. Housing would begin to improve. Jobs would be created in every sector. Right now no one is taking a chance to do any growth and building. We are all a standstill because of the national debt.

It seems to me that our President has no intentions whatsoever of slowing down the spending. Now he has promised more money that we don't have. The Federal Reserve will just keep printing more and more money until the dollar isn't worth the paper it's written on, literally. What's wrong with him? What's wrong with our Congress that the spending continues on and on without a conscience? STOP IT!

Does anyone have a fear that we are riding on a flume into the depths?At what point will the bubble burst? Will it be when the world decides that the dollar will no longer be what the world bases its monetary system on and then have it be replaced? There have been many meetings already about this. China was talking about copper money at first, now I think they have switched to silver. Gold seems to be the choice of most of the other countries. It isn't going to be the dollar that's for sure. Does Obama think the rest of the world is buying into his fantasy that the U.S. economy is ok?

Unless we get a handle on this and quickly, I can foresee riots in the streets, more crime, more hunger, more foreclosures, more layoffs, and the masses of people drowning in their own debt. Remember when in Germany you could have a barrel full of money and only be able to buy a loaf of bread? I didn't live in those times, but I sure was taught about those times in history class. Ask your great-grandparents. They can tell you how bad it can get.

I never appreciated how wonderful it was when all I had to worry about was whether we would be able to go on vacation for a little longer than we had planned.

What's a vacation? I have almost forgotten what that means? A trip to the bank, gas station,  and to the supermarket is all the traveling I do. Vacation is out of the picture altogether. Vacation sounds like a foreign word to me anymore.

How sad for our children that we can't even talk

about staying at Disneyland or going on a family trip. It isn't going to get any better in the near future. Do you remember how excited you got when vacation was mentioned? Another American dream doused with water.

When will our leaders get the wake up call? How come they can't reach an agreement on anything? These people we elected are supposed to be watching out for us. Some of them can't get past their own greed to worry about anyone else. Too much government, too much corruption. This has got change and quickly.

Chapter Nine

## WHAT STOCKS DO YOU OWN?

The Stock Market is wild. I did some day trading for a while, but let me tell you what was happening. I spent half the night listening to whatever information I could get about what was going on in the rest of the world and the other half listening to commentaries from financial experts. I came to the conclusion that they don't know either.

We have all those scandals going on there, too. Insider trading, huge sell offs by billionaires, speculators running up the oil prices, just lots of corruption.

If a politician was found to have done something unethical or immoral, the stock market would fall. If the dollar weakened there would be a big sell off and gold and silver would rise. Every week when the newest unemployment figures came out the market usually dropped. For no reason at all the stocks would skyrocket only to plummet the next day.

Every international event sent it soaring upward or plummeting. Every scandal made it go crazy. What a roller coaster ride! I finally decided I didn't have the stomach for it. My ulcers were screaming for me to get out of it. The good Lord let me sell out just before the big plunge. Thanks for that. I can't afford to lose a dime.

So, if you're limited like I am, especially after my divorce settlement, then what the heck do you do with any investment money? Housing sucks, the money markets don't pay anything, savings accounts are a joke, so what do you do? Precious metals helped for a while, but you can't just purchase them and have them pay you any income when you own the real physical metals. There is no good answer. There's nothing great out there. The Stock Market has had a good run, but I think it's days are real limited.

I put my money into buying a house for rental. It will be worth 10% less by the time it is built. There are some great buys out there, but who knows if that was the smart thing to do. If America goes bankrupt we will all be in the same boat so I don't know how that will work out.  Heaven only knows.

If you can stand the ups and downs, the roller coaster ride, then more power to you. I think the Market is designed for people who have money to gamble with, win or lose. The average Joe can't stand the loss. Bless you if you can do it

## Chapter Ten

## <u>SPARE THE ROD?</u>

Was I an abused child? Absolutely not. My Dad had an old Army belt. Oh, don't get too up righteous now, he didn't use it on me but three times in my entire life. I deserved it all three times. He would hit my butt once and that's all it took. I wasn't bruised and it didn't leave a mark anywhere but on my conscience. I hated disappointing my Dad and Mom, especially my Dad.

Funny, he had this big nerve on his forehead that would get real raised up when he was at the boiling point. My brother and I knew just when to stop pushing so hard if we saw that vein. Three times it was too late for me.

Lying was almost a sin in our house. That's what I got one spanking for, a real whopper. I don't think I ever lied again, honestly. If I ever entertained the thought of making up a whopper I would think about that and reconsider. The look on my Dad's face would be such a deterrent. I hated the disappointed look.

I don't remember what prompted me to tell Mom and Dad that I was running away from home. Vaguely, I remember something to do with my invisible rabbit. I mouthed off about every-thing I didn't like about them, the rules, and started to pull my clothes out of the closet to pack. Dad said he would get me a suitcase and help me pack. He said that if I left I would not be coming back unless I apologized for what I had said and agreed to live by the house rules. He, also, said I then would get a spanking.

It was all I could do to lift the stuffed suitcase. Dad opened the front door for me and watched me struggle to drag the suitcase down the steps. I went two doors down from our house and sat on the neighbor's steps for two hours. They came out and talked to me, but said that I should go home, I couldn't move in with them because their house was full already. I'm certain she called my folks.

After much consideration I decided to head back home. I knocked on the locked door and Dad opened it wide for me. He stood there waiting for the apology, which he got. He told me to go to my room and get ready for my spanking. I don't think I ever wanted to get a spanking so bad. I knew that it would be over quickly and that I would be a part of the family again. I was home and they loved me. That was spanking number two.

One time I was babysitting my brother while Mom

and Dad ran an errand. He was eight years younger than I was. I was instructed to have him come in from play at a certain time, that's when the third spanking event happened.

That twerp brother of mine had just gotten this bullwhip and was practicing snapping it in the front yard. When I told him he had to come in he started popping it by my feet. Of course, I'm saying that he better mind me because Mom and Dad said he was supposed to listen to me. Yea, right.

The third time he popped that bullwhip it struck my leg and hurt like heck. I snatched the whip with my brother attached, dragged him kicking and screaming into the house. About that time my parents arrived. When they walked in they found my brother on the floor, hog-tied, with me sitting on top of him yelling, getting ready to stick a sock in his mouth. It wasn't a pretty sight.

Dad grabbed me off, told me to go to my room and that he would be there shortly. I got the "you are bigger than your brother, you could have hurt him" routine. By then the mark on my leg had almost disappeared totally so I didn't have much proof of what had really happened. I got the spanking and my brother got a lecture on how he was supposed to mind me.

I am over sixty years old and I can remember exactly how many spankings I got and why I got them. I never thought my Dad was mean or cruel or abused me. I'm sure that system would not work for everyone, but it worked for me and my twerp brother. I think we both turned out to be pretty responsible, loving parents and good American citizens with strong religious beliefs.

I have to tell you what Mom would do when she got mad. Oh sure, she would use the old "wait until your Father gets home" threat, but then she did her own spanking, too. Back then we always had a paddle from one of those games you played that had a piece of elastic with a ball on it attached to a paddle. The object of the game was to hit the ball as many times as you could.

We always had one around that didn't have a ball or string left on it. It made a great spanker except that the handle would break off almost immediately, first swipe. Then there was the cheap plastic hair brush that would do the same thing. It didn't matter, one swipe and Mom was done. My brother and I would laugh behind her back when they broke. We still think it's funny.

Heaven forbid, if they had done that today, they

would be in jail and my brother and I would have been in foster homes. Kids have learned to work the system, too. They know all about child abuse, which is good, but not when they use it to threaten their parents when they need correcting. That happens.

Kids nowadays call it punishment when their laptop computer or their phones get taken away for an hour or two. Parents seem to be too lenient any more. The punishment doesn't fit the crime. I'm not abdicating beating your kid to a pulp, but I think we've gone a little overboard to the left.

I remember when my son was three years old and we were walking into a huge department store in Atlanta. Just inside the sliding doors he threw himself on the ground and began loudly screaming and he was kicking like crazy. This went on for a minute or two. I couldn't quiet him down. About that time I looked up and saw the fitting room in the men's department. I asked the clerk if I could go into one of the rooms, all the while trying to control a wild child. The clerk then pointed to the room. I went in, bopped him on the butt, got my son's attention, he stopped immediately, and we walked out quietly together.

Even back then you heard conflicting remarks from other shoppers. On the way into the men's dressing room I heard some people saying, "Good grief, why doesn't she spank him?" And on the way out I heard, "Can you believe she spanked him?" Guess what folks? That was his first and last temper tantrum. It worked for me.

I don't see the evidence of kids showing the respect we had for our parents as much any-more. There are some very nice kids out there, but do you see that more often than you see the disrespectful children? Somewhere along the line we became our kids friends and not their parents. You can be both.

No one has the time to parent like we did either. The Moms were usually home when the kids came home from school. You shared what had happened in their school day and were more into their lives. We usually let them play until a certain time then made them do their homework. Moms today have jobs to help make ends meet and have a million things to do when they get home. I truly think that has a lot to do with our kids attitudes toward us now. It isn't that we don't care, it's that our time is so limited to get every-thing done.

Even though I was raised in the South, I had to learn to have manners. Kids nowadays don't try to practice good manners. I can't tell you why they don't. Our society doesn't require them to do it so much now. You don't say sir and ma'am anymore. You talk all over everybody else during an adult family conversation. There's no "inside" voice, it's all loud. Who's to blame? We all are. It all comes back to how we treat each other.

Our kids have too much, too soon. Since when does a child eight years old need a cell phone? How on earth did we ever get to where we can not function without the cell phone? How come? Probably because when we said I'll pick you up at whatever, we were there. Somebody knew where they were supposed to be and somebody better be there. We had a routine that you stuck to no matter what. Today we are a fly by the seat of your pants society. We change plans on the spur of a minute. We have become a society of convenience.

So, do I believe in sparing the rod? No, not when it can be done reasonably. If it can't then that shouldn't be the punishment of choice.

Am I sorry for how my parents raised me with the "rod"? Nope. Not a minute spent on thinking that at all. I didn't fear my parents, I dreaded disappointing them. More than once, I changed my mind about doing the things that might have caused me to get spanked. It worked for me.

Kids don't seem to have chores to do like we did either. I earned an allowance by doing my chores. I got punished if I didn't. My butt was grounded more than once. We had a check off chart on the back of the doors in our bedroom. I was always saving up for something so I wanted to get my allowance. I didn't like it much when I didn't and soon learned it was just a lot easier to do the darn chores.

Chapter Eleven

## WHAT'S FOR DINNER?

Nothing has changed more since I was a kid than the food we eat and how we fix it. My Mom was not a great cook. But she was a master at taking one pound of hamburger and feeding four of us. She could take one tomato and slice it so thin you could read through it. We had to make things stretch.

We always had lots of sweets around. Cakes were cheap and we had lots of cookies, too, because you could get a lot of mileage out of them. Our favorite cookie was the snickerdoodle. Oh man, you made the dough into little balls and then rolled them in a mixture of cinnamon and sugar. Oh geez, they were so good. My brother and I used to eat more rolled balls than would make it on the baking sheet. Licking the bowls and spoons from the cakes and eating the dough from the cookies was the best part of helping cook them. My brother and I often fought over the "right" to first position.

Mom would take these cheap canned biscuits and poke a hole in the middle of each biscuit. We would have a bag with cinnamon and sugar in it and shake the biscuits and the holes in there to coat them. She had this little fryer and would fry them up. They were the absolute best donuts in the world. Pillsbury had nothing on Mom when it came to sweets.

We were meat and potato people. Mom could bread a meatloaf and make it last for two meals. Hotdogs and hamburgers were staples. She would split a hotdog, put cheese in it, wrap bacon around it and broil it in the oven. That was a dinner. That and baked beans and her special potato salad. Her potato salad was great.

Every morning started off with some bacon and eggs, orange juice, milk, and toast. We ate together and each of us had a part in breakfast. I hated doing bacon because I always got popped by hot grease. Finally, I learned how to fry bacon without injuries. You were full and ready for the day. On the weekends we would have time to fix grits. Butter and grits. Yum!

My Grandfather, who was six feet four inches and about 350 pounds most of his life, ate bacon and eggs every single morning until he died at 86. He put salt pork in his vegetables and ate butter on his grits. He grew his own vegetables and had fruit trees in his back yard. What a man he was! We called him Grumpy. He was the kindest most loving grand-father a kid could have. My Grandmother, Grandhoney, was the perfect match for him. She was a little lady with a big voice. She could stand her ground with anyone. Grandhoney and I were great friends.

Mom never learned to cook many vegetables. We ate lots of canned peas, beans, potatoes, squash, tomatoes, and salad. I don't think Dad much cared for many vegetables and that's why we didn't eat them. I had to learn how to cook them on my own.

If you even mention bacon to people now, they get all bent out of shape. And sweets, wow, don't talk about it. How come our grandparents and our parents all lived to ripe old ages eating things like that? How come I wasn't fat as a kid? I wonder if it has some-thing to do with all the darn chemicals and preservatives we put in our foods now. I have had two dogs die of cancer. I never heard of a dog dying of cancer when I grew up. The chemicals are killing them, too. Have we really improved our foods?

The main difference I see between kids today and kids back then is that we played outside a lot. When we came in for dinner we were tired and dirty. We didn't look pale and frail like some kids today. And then we had physical education in school. You had to have a pretty darn good excuse why you couldn't play or participate. Kids spend too much time inside. Maybe they would run off some of that mischievous behavior if they were outside playing. We sure did. We were too tired when we came in to get into trouble. We ate dinner, did our homework, took our baths and watched a little tv. And I'm not talking about sex filled thrillers either. Heck, you couldn't even show married adults sleeping in the same bed, unlike today where they show EVERYTHING. Nothing is left to the imagination anymore. Is this healthy?

I have fought my weight problem for so many years it's not funny. I eat cereal for breakfast with 2% milk, a sandwich for lunch, and a diet tv dinner for supper. I may have a dessert once in a while. I don't drink. Never smoked or done drugs. How come I'm fat? I blame what my food is made of and how it's been packaged. I cooked for thirty eight married years. I'm divorced and don't want to cook anymore than I have to now.

We are genetically altering our foods. That's scary to me. It makes me think I'm going to eat a potato sometime and have beans inside it. Who knows? Maybe all this is good for us, but I'm having trouble with it. I'm a corn and potatoes girl myself. I like my greens with a little vinegar, not something that looks like pond algae. Scary!

Our society has gotten fatter year by year, it's true. Our children are heavier than we were but I think that's inactivity not so much the food. Did you see the news the other day that some caféterias want to put up cameras to show you what your kid eats?

Now Big Brother wants to watch our kids and tell us what to feed them. School lunches should be suspended. Let me pack my kids lunch, thank you. The school's aren't serving better foods because it's too expensive for them. They make more money off of candy bars. We survived off of sandwiches packed by our Moms. What happened to that?

Our fast food restaurants are not solely to blame either. Does someone force you to drive into that window and order something unhealthy for your kid? Nope, I don't think so. Everything has now become a matter of personal choice. We need to make better choices not easier choices. Maybe it's that food has become our nation's "soother", our chocolate.

Lord knows, we have plenty of issues to worry about. Food becomes our gratification. We can't afford to have fun anymore, it costs too much, so we eat.

It's true, something must be done. We all know that

we do need to eat better, healthier. We know pretty much what we should be eating. Although one day they announce eggs are bad and the next they are good for you. Look at coffee and butter. So many things have been put on the list of healthy foods only to be taken off later. It does get a little confusing. Our waistlines are expanding and inflating just like our national debt. Things have to change.

Chapter Twelve

## THE END OF THE WORLD?

Do I think it's the end of the world? No, but I think it's the end of our Western way of life as we know it. If you think about what has changed since 2001, that's the beginning of the big turn of events. That's when we weren't safe anymore here or abroad. That's when you began to look at everyone a little differently. There has been a huge down turn in how we all feel.

What happened to the days we used to let our children play outside without worrying about some nut bothering them? What happened to leaving your doors unlocked and the keys in your car? What happened to letting your kids go to a movie or the shopping mall with their friends? What happened to the days when we watched silly programs on tv and felt good and happy after watching them? What happened to neighborhood barbeques and ice cream socials? Where's the Welcome Wagon? What happened to the family dinner where we would all be there swapping tales? What happened to the pride we all felt about everything we owned and had worked hard to get? Where are those good ole days?

If you miss those things, then good, you must be

around my age. That's when we lived happily. Oh sure, we had our cold wars and bomb shelters, but the rest of the times we were so happy. How do we get it back? How do we go back there? I'm not sure we ever can. I think those days are long gone.

Do I think it's going to get better? No, not unless we all do something to make it different. Not until we start to care about each other again will we capture some part of the old days. Do you know your next door neighbor's name? Do you have each other's phone number in case you need each other's help? Would you help them?

Can you put together a block party where everyone brings something to eat and you share recipes? Can you take the time to send a little invitation to do it and pick a day you think might work? Sure you can. Maybe only a few people will respond the first time, but the next time I guarantee you'll have more show up.

We've become a such a nation of strangers. We're all so busy doing our own thing that we are oblivious to our surroundings. Everybody is worried about making it happen. I am, too, but there is a boundary line that has to be crossed. We have to try to sincerely care about each other again.

Do you know someone on your street that needs their house painted or the yard spruced up some? Do you know if they can't physically or financially manage to take care of it themselves? Have you ever done something to help someone you know needs the help but is too proud to ask for it? We used to be a nation of neighborhoods where we all pitched in to help. What happened?

The Glenn Beck Show on Fox News has given me so much to think about. At first when I started to watch him, I thought he might be some kind of nut. Sorry, Glenn. After watching him for years, you listen to what he has to say and it begins to make sense. No wonder Fox News is the most trusted and watched news channel.

Glenn tells you like it is. He makes no apologies for what he says. And guess what, he's right on with his predictions. It's coming to bear exactly as he said it would.

He has built his case and proven he knows what he is talking about. His antics make him very entertaining, but don't ever think this reformed alcoholic doesn't know what he's talking about. He is a very intelligent man, self taught or not. He has wonderful researchers working for him to give you the facts. He warns you to make up your own mind, do your own research. That's exactly what I've done. It's been uncanny how many things have come to pass that he's predicted.

This year he has finished informing you as to what's to come. Now he's telling you what we can do about it. It's not too late to change our course. It takes courage, hope, education, faith and determination to make it happen. He has made a believer out of me.

We need that sense of family again. We need to bring God back into our lives. No, I'm not a Jesus freak. I am a Christian who trusts in God and believes that is one of the things that is missing from our lives. We need that caring and camaraderie we should feel toward our friends and neighbors . We need to teach our children manners and respect for others. Do they know they it can feel good to help someone without being paid to do it? Have we taught them that every-thing doesn't have a price tag with it? Not from the kids I see today. The majority of them want to know how much will they get paid. You know that's true. Who's forgotten to teach them? Are we setting a good example for them?

There are a lot of really genuine, caring people out there. Sometimes we need the encouragement of someone like that to bring it out in ourselves.

Take a good hard look at yourself and ask yourself if you are pleased with your contribution to this life you are given. Are you pleased with how you've been to your children or your family? Is there something you can do to make it better? Chances are there is. Think about it. Do something about it.

What could be the end of the world as we know it can be turned around to be a new beginning. It's not too late. This is a plea to do your part to make it happen. Talk to other people about it. It's not a shameful or an embarrassing discussion to have. You'll find more people who are thinking the same thing you are more than likely. Don't be afraid to do it. You won't look foolish. You will look like you care enough to want a change.

Please help me and millions of others to make this change happen. We can make a difference. We have to make a difference. We owe it to our children.

Not the end...just the beginning.

www.ingramcontent.com/pod-product-compliance
Lightning Source LLC
Chambersburg PA
CBHW020243290526

45784CB00003B/1087